We the People: Government in America

By
DANIEL S. CAMPAGNA, Ph.D.

COPYRIGHT © 2002 Mark Twain Media, Inc.

ISBN 10-digit: 1-58037-204-X
        13-digit: 978-1-58037-204-6

Printing No. CD-1550

Mark Twain Media, Inc., Publishers
Distributed by Carson-Dellosa Publishing Company, Inc.

Table of Contents

Introduction

The purpose of this book is to offer a broad overview of how the American system of government operates within the scope of a constitutional democracy.

To better familiarize the reader with this information, a varied set of instructional aids are incorporated throughout the narrative. These aids supplement, clarify, and exemplify critical and challenging aspects of the issues at hand. All terms and phrases are lucidly defined and highlighted. Numerous practical examples are included to demonstrate "how things happen" in the practice and exercise of government. To that end, the book introduces actual court cases, historical events, statistical data, hypothetical scenarios, problem-solving exercises, stimulating trivia, time line references, and similar learning tools.

Our goal is to ease the student into the complex world of government, politics, and decision-making without becoming immersed in minutiae. Although the connective theme of this book is democracy and its role within the federal government in plotting the progress of our nation, ample discussion is set aside for a review of local and state governments and politics. The reader, therefore, is introduced to numerous topics that are well structured, clearly stated, and contemporary (e.g., the terrorist attacks on the World Trade Center and the Pentagon). In doing so, we attempt to link the early founding of this nation and the creation of our government with the principles of democracy that have endured into the twenty-first century.

Time Line of Government in America

There are specific moments in time and place where things could have turned out very differently in American history and for our nation. Had we, for instance, lost the War of Independence, then it is unlikely this book would have been published! So, at various points in time, critical events occurred in our nation's history that profoundly affected the development of our government and the shaping of America. The following is a time line or chronological road map that notes these special events. Use it as a handy reference and reminder of "What happened when?" and "Who did what?". It provides a thumbnail sketch of those key moments in time and place.

DATE	EVENT
1774	The meeting of the First Continental Congress occurred.
1775	The meeting of the Second Continental Congress occurred.
1776	The Declaration of Independence was signed.
1781	The Articles of Confederation were ratified.
1783	The Treaty of Paris was signed, ending the Revolutionary War.
1787	The Constitution was written.
1789	Our nation's first president, George Washington, was sworn into office.
1791	The Bill of Rights became part of the Constitution.
1793	Democratic and Republican "societies" were founded.
1800	The nation's capital was moved to Washington, D.C.
1819	The Supreme Court ruled in the *McCulloch v. Maryland* case.
1823	The Monroe Doctrine was introduced.
1824	The Supreme Court ruled in the *Gibbons v. Ogden* case.
1846	The Mexican-American War began.
1848	The Mexican-American War ended.
1850	The Compromise of 1850 was passed.
1857	The Supreme Court ruled in the *Dred Scott* case.
1861	The Civil War began.
	The bill allowing the first federal income tax was passed.
1863	The Emancipation Proclamation was issued.
1865	The Civil War ended with the surrender of General Robert E. Lee.
1865	The Thirteenth Amendment ending slavery was added to the Constitution.
1866	The Civil Rights Act was passed.
1868	The Fourteenth Amendment was added to the Constitution.
1873	The United States experienced financial panic and national depression.
1875	The Civil Rights Act was passed (in addition to the above law).

Time Line of Government in America

1906	The Pure Food and Drug Act was passed.
1914	World War I began.
1917	The United States entered World War I.
1918	World War I ended.
1920	The Nineteenth Amendment was added to the Constitution. (Women's suffrage)
1935	The Social Security System was established.
1940	Franklin D. Roosevelt was reelected for his third term as president.
1941	The Japanese attacked Pearl Harbor; the United States entered World War II against the Axis Powers.
1944	Franklin D. Roosevelt was reelected for his fourth term as president.
1945	World War II ended.
1949	The North Atlantic Treaty Organization (NATO) was established.
1950	The Korean War began.
1953	The Korean War ended.
1954	The Vietnam War began.
1962	Soviet installation of missiles was discovered in Cuba (Cuban Missile Crisis).
1964	The Civil Rights Act was passed.
1965	The Voting Rights Act was passed.
1970	The Environmental Protection Agency was introduced.
1971	The Equal Rights Amendment was passed by Congress but failed to be ratified.
1972	The Watergate break-in occurred.
1973	The Supreme Court ruled in the *Roe v. Wade* case.
1975	The Vietnam War ended.
1980	Ronald Reagan was elected president.
1989	The Berlin Wall was torn down.
1991	The break-up of the United Soviet Socialist Republic (USSR) occurred, and the Cold War ended. The Persian Gulf War began.
1992	William J. Clinton was elected president.
1993	The Israeli and Palestinian Peace Accord was signed.
1994	Nelson Mandela was elected President of South Africa.
2000	George W. Bush was elected president.
2001	Terrorists attacked the World Trade Center and the Pentagon. All three branches of government were evacuated and relocated due to anthrax threats. The United States declared global war against terrorism. Afghanistan was invaded by Alliance troops.

Democracy

"Liberty is the right to do everything the laws permit."
—Montesquieu, 1748

The United States is a nation of over 281 million people from every country and culture. It is a nation that endorses the ideal of citizen ownership of government. We choose or elect those persons who will represent our interests in the success of government at the federal, state, and local levels. **Democracy**, therefore, is both an ideal and a concept. As such, there are several fundamental principles of democracy that best describe how it is viewed in practice.

Principles

- **Of Worth** – Everyone has value and is entitled to basic freedoms and protections accorded all citizens.
- **Rule by Law** – All citizens agree to abide by the law with no exceptions. No one may put himself or herself above or outside the law.
- **Majority Rule** – Laws must be made by the consensus of the people with considerations for the needs and interests of the minority.
- **Government as Public Servant** – Limits are placed on the type and extent of power that we give to the government, regardless of level.
- **Civil Rights** – A democratic nation provides for the rights of each citizen through laws, regulations, and elections.
- **Government by Representation** – Essential to democracy, this principle asserts the right of citizens to choose those who shall administer the government.

These principles do not mean that everyone gets to do whatever they wish. Rather, democracy is a means to an end. Freedom, equality, and representation are the means. A just and fair society is the end. What the founding fathers sought to do as they crafted the Constitution was not to repeat the earlier mistakes of rule by the British monarchy, of a society under imperial rule and without true representation.

Ours is a compromise government. It is best described as a **representative democracy**—the above principles are upheld through a system of elections, branches of government, laws, and public officials. No one person, agency, or unit of government should ever dominate the political process and deny the consensus (and rights/freedoms) of the people. Representative democracy has not always worked. There are many examples in American history where people's rights have been exploited or ignored, such as slavery, the near-extermination of the Native Americans, religious intolerance, and the suppression of civil rights. Thus, democracy remains an ongoing "process" as well as a goal. It represents the best promise of peace and order in a nation of over 281 million citizens.

The Statue of Liberty

One hundred fifty-two feet high and placed atop a 150-foot pedestal, the Statue of Liberty is perhaps the most famous symbol of democracy. It is located in Upper New York Bay on Liberty Island. The French sculptor F.A. Bartholdi designed the statue of a woman holding an uplifted torch. The statue was shipped to the United States in 1885 and dedicated in 1886. The original purpose of the Statue of Liberty was to commemorate and celebrate the American-French alliance during the Revolutionary War.

The pedestal contains the equally famous sonnet by Emma Lazarus titled:

"The New Colossus"

Give me your tired, your poor,
Your huddled masses yearning to breathe free,
The wretched refuse of your teeming shore,
Send these, the homeless, tempest-tossed, to me,
I lift my lamp beside the golden door!

This passage was written as a symbolic greeting to the waves of immigrants who made their way to American shores. Early immigrants came to the United States to find work and to escape religious or political persecution. These remain strong incentives to immigrate to America (times have not changed much!), especially for people of third world (nonindustrial) countries. For many, the Statue of Liberty is their first impression of the United States because of its easy visibility as they arrive by ship or airplane. It is, in a sense, a visual introduction to their new nation. The Statue of Liberty still represents freedom, hope, and an opportunity to participate in the future of a nation …

BUT

Given the fact that immigrants pose a very unique set of challenges and problems for society (e.g., language barriers, terrorism, illegal laborers, and crime), we must ponder this question, "Should we continue to allow so many foreigners to enter and reside within the United States?" If the Statue of Liberty truly is an invitation to the world's homeless and oppressed, then it is contradictory to deny them entrance. On the other hand, we have a long tradition of expelling undesirable aliens or citizens who had every intention of trying to overthrow the government (for example, through assassination and communism). What is your viewpoint?

_____

_____

_____

_____

The U.S. Constitution

"We the People of the United States ..." Thus begins the famous document that established our national government. For such a valuable document, it is not especially long or complex. It contains a preamble, seven articles, and twenty-seven amendments. Within the space of relatively few pages, a government, a nation, and a national identity—Americans—were born. The Constitution was framed with an eye toward "balance"; that is, it created a triad of power with three branches and three levels of government. These include the executive, legislative, and judicial branches at the federal, state, and local levels of government. Each acts as a check upon the other in order to keep some sense of balance and representation within the nation. The U.S. Supreme Court, for instance, does not tell a state governor how to run his/her state.

The Constitution is based on a handful of basic principles or guidelines. These include the following ideas:

- **Separation of Powers** - The authority to govern must be spread among the three levels and branches of government.

- **Popular Rule/Sovereignty** - Our government belongs to its citizens who elect people to help run the country (e.g., judges, senators, etc.). Also, it is civilians who control the government, not the military.

- **Checks and Balances** - Each branch of government serves as a check upon the other so that no single unit has excessive power (e.g., the president cannot compel Congress to pass laws).

- **Constituency** - Elected officials are legally accountable to the people who elect them.

- **Federalism** - This is a system by which some powers are set aside for the national government, while other powers are reserved for the state and local governments. Supremacy of national laws is part of federalism.

- **Mixed Term Lengths** - Legislators have varying lengths of terms in order to maximize representation of all citizens (U.S. senators serve six years; representatives serve two years).

Did You Know That ...

■■ There have actually been TWO constitutions in our history? In 1781, the Articles of Confederation were passed. The second is our present Constitution, which was written in 1787.

■■ The Constitution is over 200 years old? September 17 is the celebrated anniversary of the signing of the Constitution.

The U.S. Constitution: Word Search

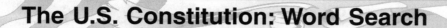

Directions: Find and circle the words listed below in the word search puzzle. Words may be printed forward, backward, up, down, or diagonally.

```
K F N G S T U Y N W Q U I  Y I  L T R O J V G D E
J A C V D T W S C Y Q F I  Q Y Q J X W T Q U M L
U N A N N I N E S R L V K A U E T J I  F H S U F
E O L E O Z H E P U D L N U M X B D B Z P Z Q R
W I  M L I  T I  X M K G F L R X E E V X R E M U E
I  T V X T H U B G D I  D P E M A R A R K V U P E
D U O V A E U R G N N T O J L J C I  T X U K S D
C T I  R T U V F O G P E N S K T B J C O N T K O
G I  M D N W R J T Y C E M E R I  J A F A H W T M
B T K S E W F Z W H C K B A M I  G L X G U J W S
Y S S M S L T V O N V F J Y S N B Y I  F Y E I  S
F N L Y E Z J X A W E Z Z U C I  R R S V V Q P Y
E O A D R I  K L B E U W V G O N F E F F N D X S
T C X R P W A X I  I  T S R W Y O J D V R R I  Z A
S T B H E B Q A Y T D P W W L C L Q N O Z Z T H
B S U P R E M E C O U R T L F C H N G T G O E U
L C X W C I  D A P Z L Q I  W G J H S Y P U S T O
J I  O I  D F T X G X T B S N B U A P S S Z F R Q
I  H B B U F A Y E Q X V V F U G A R T I  C L E S
T N D E F A O E L B M A E R P D C X G Y A K I  B
E C O I  R J B U F D L A N O I  T A N H Y O J V C
D O L Q V T M J Y N G G O M D F T M N D G V L J
Y I  A G P D Y I  N G T C U U E I  O N J Q S E X G
V M X C C O Y L S E L P I  C N I  R P S T V N A Q
```

WORD LIST

Amendments	America	Articles	Balance
Bill of Rights	Constitution	Freedoms	Government
Ideals	Liberty	National	Preamble
Principles	Representation	Supreme Court	

Name: _____   Date: _____

The U.S. Constitution: Kriss Kross

Directions: Use a pencil for this puzzle. Fit the words from the list below in the correct spaces below. There may be two words that fit in the same boxes, but if you are unable to connect the next word, you know you have written in the wrong word. Erase and continue with the other word that fits.

6 LETTERS
Ideals

7 LETTERS
America
Balance
Liberty

8 LETTERS
Articles
Freedoms
National
Preamble

10 LETTERS
Amendments
Government
Principles

12 LETTERS
Bill of Rights
Constitution
Supreme Court

14 LETTERS
Representation

The Preamble

The Preamble to the Constitution is one sentence in length. The language used in this passage is quite ordinary. It contains the fundamental goals of the fledgling government, which is a set of directives about the ideals and objectives that Americans hold near and dear to their view of democracy. There are six goals in the Preamble.

"We the people of the United States, in order to ...":

<u>Goal 1:</u> *"form a more perfect union, ..."*

Meaning: Establish a national government that would be able to more effectively run a newly-instituted nation. The Articles of Confederation simply lacked the strength to keep the states working toward a common good and prosperity.

<u>Goal 2:</u> *"establish justice, ..."*

Meaning: Provide systems and organizations within the federal and state government(s) that would insure basic fairness to citizens (e.g., protection from false accusations or imprisonment).

<u>Goal 3:</u> *"insure domestic tranquility, ..."*

Meaning: Make arrangements for the general health, welfare, and public peace of all communities (e.g., police departments, laws, rules, and regulations).

<u>Goal 4:</u> *"provide for the common defense, ..."*

Meaning: Provide the means and methods whereby our nation, its people, and its property could be protected from the threat of war or civil insurrection (e.g., standing army, national guard/state militia, weapons allowed in citizens' homes).

<u>Goal 5:</u> *"promote the general welfare, ..."*

Meaning: Roughly translated, this goal refers to the sense of well-being that citizens have about their lives and their communities. This is expressed in their right to vote, to hold general elections/public office, and their participation in the development of our society.

<u>Goal 6:</u> *"and secure the blessings of liberty to ourselves and our posterity, ..."*

Meaning: A new government, to be successful, must endure. This final goal was an assertion that the United States was an experiment in freedom that had to withstand the test of time. For generations without end, the Preamble and the Constitution would stand as protections and reminders of what our nation would strive to achieve.

" ... do ordain and establish this Constitution for the United States of America."

Lost in Space

As hard as it may be to believe or visualize, at some point a number of humans will probably be residing in gigantic space stations orbiting the earth. This will be part of a hugely complex undertaking to colonize outer space and distant planets. Nations will be searching for new sources of energy, raw minerals, and inhabitable areas for its citizens. Unlike the settling of the western frontier centuries ago, the stakes are much higher for humankind. In a sense, the "race to the stars" is a race for expansion and survival. Because the United States has a long track record of achievements in space (thanks to NASA), it is reasonable to presume that we will be looking skyward for solutions to problems that plague us on Earth, such as industrial pollution and global warming.

Laws will be necessary to govern these new space pioneers, just as they were necessary when we settled the western frontier. Wherever groups of people congregate to create an orderly society—whether it is Earth, Mars, or other extraterrestrial sites—some form of organized government and system of rules is required. It is too risky and unreasonable to expect everyone to be orderly. In the short exercise below, imagine that you have been asked to write a new preamble that would explain how these "space settlers" should be governed. Refer to the principles listed in the original Preamble as a guide.

Something to keep in mind is that life in outer space will not be like anything we would experience on Earth. There are all sorts of unanswered questions to consider. For starters, who has the right and authority to set rules for the use of outer space? What sorts of things in the existing Constitution would be useful (or useless) to the welfare of the colonists? For example, would there be any need to provide for the common defense? Or promote the general welfare?

Perhaps the biggest question to address as you draft your preamble is this: Who owns outer space and the planets? Start from that point of inquiry and develop a few simple statements that describe how your new "space nation" is to be organized. Don't worry, there is obviously no right or wrong answer to this exercise! It is meant to help you think creatively about an issue that has stumped scholars and politicians for decades. Keep in mind that whatever you decide upon, it may not please every would-be colonist. Use your own paper if you need more room.

PREAMBLE FOR A NEW "SPACE NATION"

_____

_____

_____

_____

_____

_____

The Bill of Rights

The first ten amendments to the United States Constitution are called the Bill of Rights. They were added to the Constitution in 1791 as a set of protections for citizens against potential abuses by the national government. Since then, the amendments have been used to shield citizens from transgressions by state governments as well as by the federal government. These amendments describe, in general terms, many of our essential freedoms and rights. We depend on the courts to help clarify the exact meaning and extent of these amendments.

Amendment 1: Congress shall make no law respecting an establishment of religion, or prohibiting the free exercise thereof; or abridging the freedom of speech, or of the press; or the right of the people peaceably to assemble, and to petition the government for a redress of grievances.

Summary: Freedom of religion, speech, press, assembly, and to petition the government

Amendment 2: A well-regulated militia being necessary to the security of a free State, the right of the people to keep and bear arms shall not be infringed.

Summary: The right to keep and bear arms

Amendment 3: No soldier shall, in time of peace be quartered in any house, without the consent of the owner, nor in time of war, but in a manner to be prescribed by law.

Summary: Soldiers cannot be placed in homes without the owner's consent.

Amendment 4: The right of the people to be secure in their persons, houses, papers, and effects, against unreasonable searches and seizures, shall not be violated, and no warrants shall issue but upon probable cause, supported by oath or affirmation, and particularly describing the place to be searched, and the persons or things to be seized.

Summary: This provides security from unreasonable searches and seizures; probable cause is needed for warrants.

The Bill of Rights (cont.)

Amendment 5:   No person shall be held to answer for a capital or otherwise infamous crime, unless on a presentment or indictment of a grand jury, except in cases arising in the land or naval forces, or in the militia, when in actual service in time of war or public danger; nor shall any person be subject for the same offense to be twice put in jeopardy of life or limb; nor shall be compelled in any criminal case to be a witness against himself, nor be deprived of life, liberty, or property, without due process of law; nor shall private property be taken for public use without just compensation.

Summary: No self-incrimination or double jeopardy for crimes; the right to a grand jury, due process of law, and compensation for the taking of public property

Amendment 6:   In all criminal prosecutions, the accused shall enjoy the right to a speedy and public trial, by an impartial jury of the State and district wherein the crime shall have been committed, which district shall have been previously ascertained by law, and to be informed of the nature and cause of the accusation; to be confronted with the witnesses against him; to have compulsory process for obtaining witnesses in his favor, and to have the assistance of counsel for his defense.

Summary: The right to a speedy trial by jury, to be informed of charges, to confront witnesses, and to have legal advice

Amendment 7:   In suits at common law, where the value in controversy shall exceed twenty dollars, the right of trial by jury shall be preserved, and no fact tried by a jury shall be otherwise reexamined in any court of the United States, than according to the rules of the common law.

Summary: The right to a jury trial in civil cases over twenty dollars in value

Amendment 8:   Excessive bail shall not be required, nor excessive fines imposed, nor cruel and unusual punishments inflicted.

Summary: No excessive bail or fines or cruel and unusual punishments may be imposed.

Amendment 9:   The enumeration in the Constitution, of certain rights, shall not be construed to deny or disparage others retained by the people.

Summary: The Constitution shall not deny other rights of the people.

Amendment 10:   The powers not delegated to the United States by the Constitution, nor prohibited by it to the States, are reserved to the States respectively, or to the people.

Summary: State powers are acknowledged.

"When peace has been broken anywhere, the peace of all countries everywhere is in danger."   —Franklin D. Roosevelt, 1939

Which Is Which?: The Bill of Rights

Many people think they know the Bill of Rights but often get confused over the first ten amendments and what they actually mean. Decide to which amendment in the Bill of Rights each of the following examples applies. Keep in mind that some of the examples have nothing to do with the Bill of Rights. Put the amendment number (or place a zero for "no amendment") on the line next to the example.

_____ 1. You can meet with some of your friends and go skateboarding down a public sidewalk.

_____ 2. You decide to stand on school grounds during class periods and shout out biblical passages to passersby.

_____ 3. You have the right to smoke tobacco if you want to.

_____ 4. You can be forced to submit to unreasonable searches and seizures of your property.

_____ 5. Members of the armed forces may be tried in military court under military law/justice.

_____ 6. A bail amount of $250 is set for someone accused of stealing from a department store.

_____ 7. A gun enthusiast can keep his/her collection of weapons in his/her home.

_____ 8. You are arrested for writing an editorial protesting the decisions of the local board of aldermen in your city.

_____ 9. A person can be arrested and tried repeatedly for the same crime until he/she is finally convicted.

_____ 10. Anyone charged with a crime must normally be tried in the district or area in which the crime occurred.

_____ 11. You are denied access to an airplane for which you have a valid ticket because the stewardess thinks you are drunk.

_____ 12. A state decides to start its own lottery.

_____ 13. You wear a bright orange T-shirt that reads "I Hate Bigotry."

_____ 14. If arrested for a felony or major crime, you cannot be held indefinitely in jail without going to trial.

_____ 15. You can choose which, if any, organized religion you wish to join.

_____ 16. Unpopular political views can be suppressed by the federal government.

_____ 17. Foreigners living in this country can run for public office even though they are not citizens of the United States.

_____ 18. A judge sentences to death a person convicted of tax evasion.

_____ 19. You petition the school board for longer lunches.

_____ 20. A person can dress in any manner he/she wishes in any public place.

The Amendments

There are 27 amendments to the Constitution. Of these, the most famous are the first ten amendments known as the **Bill of Rights**. Amendments are written in response to the changing times within our society. The founding fathers in 1787, for example, had no way of predicting the Civil Rights Movement, the Internet, the microchip, DNA, nuclear energy, space travel, or cloning. Yet, each of these issues has created new challenges to the government's ability to rule fairly and effectively. We rarely enact new amendments—only 27 amendments in 215 years—but when enacted, they enable our nation to keep the Constitution on course.

Since we have already examined the Bill of Rights, let's look at the other 17 amendments. Amendments 15, 19, 23, 24, and 26 extend the right to vote to all citizens including Blacks, women, 18-year-olds, and citizens of Washington, D.C., and eliminate poll taxes. Amendments 12, 17, 20, 22, and 25 address the issue of how we select the president, vice president, and members of Congress. Amendments 11, 13, 14, 16, 18, 21, and 27 deal with a variety of issues, such as banning slavery (13), the creation of a national income tax (16), and defining citizenship (14).

New amendments to the Constitution are proposed annually, but they rarely succeed. The last amendment (27) was added in 1992. To attach an amendment to the Constitution is a two-step process that requires a **proposal** and a **ratification**. There are four methods of amending the Constitution, but only one has proven successful throughout the centuries; this approach is called an **Act of Congress**. Both the Senate and the House must pass a two-thirds vote in order to approve a proposed amendment. Once that is done, the proposal must be **ratified** (approved) by three-fourths of the state legislatures within seven years. This means that 38 states must agree to ratify the amendment before the seven years are up, or it does not pass. As you can imagine, it is very difficult to generate agreement among 38 states on any proposed amendment to the Constitution.

Persons unhappy with a government decision, a court decision, or simply seeking publicity may try to put a proposal before Congress. We must, however, be sure that any change in the Constitution is legal, promotes the goals as defined in the Preamble, and is likely to benefit the majority of citizens. To do so requires a **consensus** (general agreement) of public opinion on topics that sometimes have no overwhelming support. Amending the Constitution, therefore, is a slow and extremely difficult task because any change potentially affects all citizens. Introducing an income tax, allowing citizens the right to vote, and guarding our civil rights are three examples of how amendments have altered the direction of our society in order to make the Constitution more equitable (impartial).

Federalism

Federalism is the idea that power is shared between a strong national government and the fifty states. This separation of powers applies to all levels of government. Initially, the federal government possessed very limited powers over citizens. However, two major court cases early in our nation's history changed that situation dramatically.

McCulloch v. Maryland (1819) - The U.S. Supreme Court said that the powers of the federal government are not limited solely to those powers expressly stated in the Constitution. The government, in other words, could exercise a broader range of powers over the states.

Gibbons v. Ogden (1824) - This case involved two competing steamboat firms. The U.S. Supreme Court decided that the federal government could regulate commerce involving products, people, and services. This decision gave the federal government authority to regulate businesses, industries, and commerce between states.

It can be somewhat challenging to identify which powers belong to the federal government and which powers are set aside for the states. An easy way to grasp the distinctions is by placing these powers into categories:

Category 1: DELEGATED POWERS
Defined: Powers/authority set aside for use by the federal government and its three branches
Examples: Printing currency; declaring war; weights and measures; treaties; taxation

Category 2: CONCURRENT POWERS
Defined: Powers shared by the federal government and the states
Examples: Regulating banks; establishing the criminal justice system; operating schools

Category 3: RESERVED POWERS
Defined: Powers left to the states by the federal government
Examples: Compulsory education; utilities; regulating tobacco and alcohol

Category 4: IMPLIED (INHERENT) POWERS
Defined: Powers that are logically derived from delegated powers
Examples: Creating national banks; administering federal lands; space travel

Category 5: PROHIBITED (RESTRICTED) POWERS
Defined: Powers that neither the federal government nor the states can use
Examples: Bill of attainder; ex post facto laws; suspending writ of habeas corpus

Name: _____ Date: _____

Federalism: Word Search

Directions: Find and circle the words listed below in the word search puzzle. Words may be printed forward, backward, up, down, or diagonally.

```
N Z C Z X H S R E W O P F O N O I T A R A P E S
J K Y K M N W D F M P X L U X S P M V A W N Y Q
M O Y B M K J T P M N Y N P R E J Q Q I E D N P
X S C I T I L O P T C X M K L H B N P R Y A K T
C W L P F T Q X M K B J S P F C Z O R Q L P Y J
M Q R B J H T U G M A T I V P N V I M K N N U C
Y L E N I J P R Z Q C G L K Z A K T O Q O E B F
U V S Q G N A C B N B S A Q M R D U N D I S X D
Z O E U P R O Z N U U S N X J B P T Q A T B N E
A R R R X D F S F F P C O S I R Y I A Q A W B L
H U V U L W W F A U I R I Y X B O T M S N D J E
Q V E S K A X O P L P T T R N Z X S Z F E N B G
D R D G Q L L Q B U P U A C G I O N K S N Q X A
H T P V P F O U Y T K H N G O Q K O O V O I O T
V R O J T O P Q B N A B N L P C F C L H S V W E
B L W O U E B J W M A N Y S T A T E S C S W O D
J R E I R L S M L V D V S D Y C A R C O M E D P
U O R S H U R Q J O L V Q S G F R R N S J B N O
A W S Z B R R B O D Y V N B F L E J L H D Q T W
S E C N A L A B D N A S K C E H C Y D W Q R F E
C Q M K V S P O U I X F Q T N E M N R E V O G R
V B O Y V N B R A U N W S S N G B V H Z N D N S
E L R H E E R S R E W O P D E I L P M I Y A J T
C G X G E Q L H V U X B P N X M Q I G E M V A D
```

WORD LIST

Checks and Balances	Branches	Constitution	Delegated Powers
Democracy	Government	Implied Powers	Many States
Nationalism	One Nation	Politics	Republic
Reserved Powers	Rule of Law	Separation of Powers	

Name: _____ Date: _____

The Principles of Government: Cryptogram

Directions: Decipher the words below that relate to the basic principles of American government. Use the master key provided on page 18. Substitute the letter given in the clue with the corresponding letter in the master key.

1. A one-sentence introduction to the Constitution

 ___ ___ ___ ___ ___ ___ ___ ___ ___
  C   E   R   N   Z   O   Y   R

2. The document that formed the government

 ___ ___ ___ ___ ___ ___ ___ ___ ___ ___ ___ ___
  P   B   A   F   G   V   G   H   G   V   B   A

3. The first ten amendments to the Constitution are called the _____. (three words)

 ___ ___ ___ ___ ___ ___ ___ ___ ___ ___ ___ ___
  O   V   Y   Y   B   S   E   V   T   U   G   F

4. _____ powers are shared by the federal government and the states.

 ___ ___ ___ ___ ___ ___ ___ ___ ___ ___
  P   B   A   P   H   E   E   R   A   G

5. A method for amending the Constitution (three words) ___ ___ ___
                                                         N   P   G

 ___ ___ ___ ___ ___ ___ ___ ___ ___ ___
  B   O   P   B   A   T   E   R   F   F

6. Persons who drafted the Constitution (two words)

 ___ ___ ___ ___ ___ ___ ___ ___
  S   B   H   A   Q   V   A   T

 ___ ___ ___ ___ ___ ___ ___
  S   N   G   U   R   E   F

Alexander
Hamilton

Benjamin
Franklin

James
Madison

Name: _____ Date: _____

 ## The Principles of Government: Cryptogram (cont.)

7. A basic principle of democracy

   __ __ __ __ __ __ __ __
   R D H N Y V G L

8. Additions to the Constitution

   __ __ __ __ __ __ __ __ __ __
   N Z R A Q Z R A G F

9. The idea that no person is above or outside the law (three words)

   __ __ __ __ __ __ __ __ __
   E H Y R B S Y N J

10. The principle that the government belongs to the people (two words)

    __ __ __ __ __ __ __   __ __ __ __
    C B C H Y N E   E H Y R

11. The people to whom elected officials are accountable

    __ __ __ __ __ __ __ __ __ __ __ __
    P B A F G V G H R A P L

12. A term for the sections of the Constitution

    __ __ __ __ __ __ __ __
    N E G V P Y R F

A	B	C	D	E	F	G	H	I	J	K	L	M
N	O	P	Q	R	S	T	U	V	W	X	Y	Z
N	O	P	Q	R	S	T	U	V	W	X	Y	Z
A	B	C	D	E	F	G	H	I	J	K	L	M

The Liberty Bell

"Proclaim Liberty throughout all the land unto all the inhabitants thereof ..."

The above statement from Leviticus 25:10 is inscribed on the famous Liberty Bell. The Liberty Bell is one of the great symbols of American democracy. Like the Statue of Liberty, it has become associated with our nation's struggle for independence and a declaration of our freedom. The Liberty Bell, however, has a curious history. The State Assembly of Pennsylvania ordered a bell (made in England) to be cast and placed in what is now called Independence Hall.

It arrived in Philadelphia in 1753 and was positioned for a sound test. Shortly after, the bell cracked. A patch job was tried on the brittle bell by applying extra copper. This time, in the same year, the bell was rung but the tone was considered "off." It did not have the quality and resonance that people had expected. Two repairmen, Pass and Stow, recast the bell, basically starting from scratch.

Again the 2,080-pound bell was raised in the belfry, rung, and proved to be a disappointment. An order was placed by the State Assembly to the original foundry to make a new bell. Upon its arrival, the citizens/assemblymen discovered that the new bell was not a superior version of the old bell. So the old bell was left hanging in the steeple of Independence Hall. The newer bell was stored on the roof of the State House. Since then, the Liberty Bell has been rung for many important events:

- King George III assumed the throne of England. (1761)
- The First Continental Congress (1774)
- The battles of Concord and Lexington (1775)
- The Declaration of Independence (1776)
- To commemorate George Washington's birthday
- The Fourth of July (tapped lightly, not rung)

Some citizens complained that the bell was too intrusive and noisy. Others said the bell was more of a nuisance than a help. The great bell had been repaired, recast, hidden from British soldiers, and finally rendered unusable in 1846. The crack, which had developed throughout past decades, had reached a stage where further ringing would destroy the bell. By that time the Liberty Bell was seen as a symbol of freedom. The first recognized use of the term Liberty Bell is generally associated with the publication of an antislavery poem of the same name from the mid-1800s. The significance of the Liberty Bell is what it has come to represent in the minds of citizens—something of immense historical and national value. Certainly, no one in 1751 could have anticipated the lasting importance of the purchase order for a rather ordinary bell that was transformed into a permanent icon of American history.

Citizenship

"The first requisite of a good citizen in this Republic of ours is that he shall be able and willing to pull his weight."
—Theodore Roosevelt

Being a citizen of the United States involves rights, obligations, and a promise of loyalty. As President Theodore Roosevelt noted above, each citizen is expected to participate in the success of the country. This can be accomplished through such acts as voting, paying taxes, joining the armed forces, and running for public office. However, you must be a citizen first; a person can become a citizen through several methods. The most common is known as **"jus soli,"** a term that means <u>where</u> a person is born usually decides his/her citizenship. A person born in America is an American citizen. Another way is called **"jus sanguinis,"** which means that one earns citizenship by <u>blood</u>. Any child who is born to American citizens becomes an American. The law normally, but not always, recognizes the citizenship of the father in making the determination.

A third and often controversial method is labeled **naturalization**. Naturalization is the process and procedure by which we grant citizenship to immigrants. It must be a voluntary decision by the immigrant—the government cannot and will not compel anyone to become a citizen. These interested persons must comply with several specific requirements for citizenship:

- Five-year residency in the United States (three-year residency if married to an American citizen)
- Must possess "good moral character"
- Must be at least 18 years of age
- Must read, write, and speak English
- Must comprehend U.S. government and history

Children under 18 automatically qualify as American citizens once their parents are naturalized. Permanent (fixed) entry into this country is generally restricted to those who are eligible to become citizens. Exceptions are made for political/war refugees, former allies, humanitarian requests, and other equally pressing needs.

Until a person is naturalized and becomes a citizen, he/she is listed as an alien. A **resident alien** is a foreign citizen who resides permanently in this country and intends to become a citizen. That person is willing to surrender his/her previous citizenship to another nation. A **non-resident alien** is a foreigner who lives in the United States for a period of time (e.g., a student before returning to his/her native country). An **illegal alien** is, quite simply, someone who enters and lives in America illegally (without permission).

Elections

An **election** is a process and a procedure. It is used to select people for office and to decide issues of importance, such as passing a bond to build a new school. Elections occur at all three levels of government. A person may, for example, vote for an alderman (local), a governor (state), and a senator (national) in the same election. Only eligible citizens may vote in an election. A qualified citizen must be at least 18 years old to register to vote in an election.

The length of office for an elected official varies and is called a **term**. The President may only serve two terms of four years each. U.S. Senators are in office for six years, and U.S. Representatives serve two years. The actual elections also vary as to when they are held—it depends on what level of government is holding the election. Normally, for example, each state decides when an election may be conducted. At the national level, however, elections always occur on the first Tuesday following the first Monday in the month of November in even-numbered years.

There are different types of elections. Ours is essentially a two-party system consisting of Democrats and Republicans. Before the general election, a **primary election** may be held. Registered voters are provided the chance to choose which candidates of their respective party will run in the general election. This is known as a **closed primary**. Democrats choose Democratic candidates, and Republicans choose Republican candidates. An **open primary** allows a voter to pick a party at the polling site. A **blanket primary** means that a voter can vote for different candidates across party lines for different offices. Do not worry about keeping these distinctions in order. Most primaries are of the closed type. It is the **general election** that decides who wins after a primary. Sometimes a **special election** is ordered when a vacancy occurs, such as in the House of Representatives, due to illness or retirement. The winner then completes the remainder of the term. As a handy rule of thumb, it is worth noting that in national elections, the **incumbent** or person currently in office will almost always win reelection. For many reasons, an incumbent enjoys a huge advantage over challengers in any upcoming election.

On election day, registered voters go to a **polling** or voting site. They cast their votes by using one of the following methods: a paper ballot, depositing a specific marker into a container or voter box, or a computer punch card. The vote is recorded by voting judges, and a tally is kept to decide the winner. The results are then tabulated, certified by public officials, and announced. The winner(s) are later sworn into office prior to assuming their new duties. The election process may appear fairly simple, but running for office is not. An election campaign, as we shall see in the next section, can be a wild business as candidates jockey for the media's and voters' attention in order to gain popular support.

Name: _____ Date: _____

Elections: Word Search

Directions: Find and circle the words listed below in the word search puzzle. Words may be printed forward, backward, up, down, or diagonally.

```
L S W R L C Z T A P T Q S E I T R A P D R I H T
M B E E K R V R B R N P Q A R N I D N Y X X U S
A S S S V J O D A M U J Y L W N S O F G E W W L
G N I U Q I Y F B C O H Y E S Z I H V G L K H F
D B L L W N Q N N C F T A G T F V V S E H P P
Q I F T L B M T D H E O A S A K N P U O C K G G
W B J S Q O J U H T R X M N N O B S V N T G E Q
C O N V E N T I O N C I I B K F N X X Z O W Q U
Z Y Z A H A A Z J D Q M A G U E K X O X R E N U
U U R B L N M P F P O T V T S N J I Z Z A H I I
G C G H O G L C H N E L P N T N E D E P L S D Y
T B G W G T F I J A L V O C I V M K V I C E J Y
K F J F Z Y B O Z H I C E B Q G O L I W O O S V
B C W P K A S B A V J E L W B W M G J L L T O G
R Y C V L W B R Y R S O U U N J O E O U L L C T
V E L L C A M X L W S Z Z P D H Z G P Q E Z G A
G T O R S E I T R A P L R T R E Y U M T G A H I
Y T H B W V I E H Y W Z O W V I J Q L R E O S D
B K S M B J Z F G F F S T M E J M T D T A L S E
G E R R Y M A N D E R I N G O M C A K L T Y Y M
Z Y H P U D A V T U X V Y F V V O A R O Z L C S
L T H V P K L D O E L E C T O R A T E Y Z N S S
J L A N Q N Z Y I W C G Y N H K S W I F C B R A
D S B U E K J I G S E G S P L I T T I C K E T M
```

WORD LIST

Ballot	Consensus	Convention	Electoral College
Electorate	Gerrymandering	Ideology	Mass Media
Nomination	Parties	Primary	Recount
Results	Split Ticket	Third Parties	

The Electoral College

The Electoral College is an often misunderstood and confusing topic. Article II, Section 1 of the Constitution set up the Electoral College as a type of compromise. Every four years on the first Tuesday after the first Monday in November, we vote for a president and a vice president. What may confuse people is the fact that we do not technically vote directly for the candidates! We vote for electors. The electors, in turn, vote for the candidates. They are supposed to vote or endorse the candidate who wins the majority of the popular vote. There are 538 electors in the College; this number equals the total of U.S. Senators and U.S. Representatives per state, plus three electors for Washington, D.C. On the Monday after the second Wednesday in December, the electors convene at their respective state capitols. It is there that they vote for the office of president and vice president. On January 6, the President of the Senate opens the results and announces the final vote of the Electoral College to the House of Representatives and the Senate.

On January 20, the winning candidates are sworn into office. However, there are some interesting "glitches" in this process. Normally, the electors vote for the candidate who wins the popular vote in his or her state. It is still possible, however, for a candidate to win the total popular vote, yet lose the election. This is one of the major criticisms of the Electoral College. A second problem is equal representation. Regardless of size, every state is given at least three electoral votes. Small states, therefore, have disproportionate influence. Large states, on the other hand, receive the lion's share of electoral votes. By winning about one dozen of the largest states, a candidate can win the presidency. Thus, a candidate will try to acquire the popular vote of "big" states, such as California, Florida, and Texas.

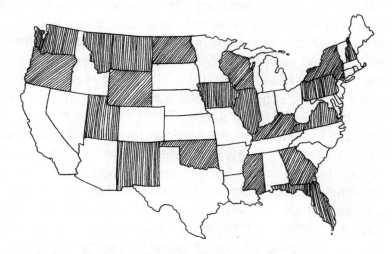

The winner needs 270 votes in the Electoral College. If neither side gets a majority of electoral votes, the issue is decided by ballot in the House of Representatives. Each state is allotted one vote to cast for the candidate of their choice. In 1800, for example, the House of Representatives voted 53 times to break a tie before finally choosing Thomas Jefferson as president! In the election of 2000, there was widespread debate about whether Democrat Al Gore or Republican George W. Bush actually won the popular (and electoral) vote in the swing state of Florida.

Did You Know That ...

 President Rutherford B. Hayes won the election of 1876 over Samuel Tilden by a one-vote margin in the Electoral College. However, President Hayes LOST the popular vote by a margin of 264,000 votes!

The Ballot

Let us assume that someone is an 18-year-old citizen of the United States and is qualified to vote in an election. To be qualified also means that a person has **registered** as a voter in his/her district or precinct. Registration means a person "signs up" to vote and provides proof of residency in the state and district. A specific **polling place** (voting place) will be assigned to that registered voter. He or she must go to that place to vote in all elections—national, state, and local.

Let us go a step further—an election is approaching. The voter goes to the polling place ready to cast his/her vote. **Poll watchers** (inspectors) may be standing about to make sure that no one interferes with the voter. What should the voter expect to happen after entering the polling place? After signing in, the voter will be handed a **ballot** by the election judges and directed towards a curtained booth. A ballot is the means by which we cast our votes. It is either a piece of paper or an electronic ballot. The paper ballot is just that—a page or more of candidates listed by political party and office. A voter chooses candidates by pencil, mark, or similar method. The finished ballot is placed into a secured voting box. Electronic voting uses a voting machine that has either small levers or a punch pen. The most common version is an **automatic voting device** that has punch cards. Votes are electronically collected and counted. The punch card, like the paper ballot, is returned to the election judge(s). There are other arrangements for voting that depend on the state's election laws.

The United States adopted the **Australian ballot** as its generic means for casting votes. We use the Australian ballot for several excellent reasons. First, ballots are copied at taxpayer expense (no private interests allowed). Early ballots in America were color-coded and easily distinguishable from one another. Voters had no freedom of choice or privacy. This practice encouraged corruption. Second, voting is secret, a practice that is believed to originate in Salem, Massachusetts, in 1629. The point is simple—no one is entitled to know how someone votes in an election. There is little or no point in voting if ballots are "rigged," and we cannot expect our vote to be secret. Third, officials conduct the elections. This practice prevents the perils of outside interests meddling with the voters and the ballots. A final benefit of the Australian ballot is uniformity. Each ballot is the same in format and appearance. Each election is held in the same manner. A voter has a choice in his selections: **straight ticket** or **split ticket.** The straight ticket is a decision to vote for **all** of the candidates of one political party. A split ticket, as the name implies, means that a voter can pick candidates from both political parties (but not for the same office). At the end of the election day, usually in early evening, the votes are tallied. The results are announced either that same day or on the next day in the event of a close race or a contested election.

To Win, You've Got to Run!

Imagine that you have decided to run for public office. The desire to serve the electorate, your fellow citizens, is strong. You want to be the sort of public servant that Thomas Jefferson would appreciate. Let us further assume that you have chosen the office of state representative as your target. The problem is that you are a political rookie. You are clueless about what to do and what to expect. Relax! This brief walk through the election process could (perhaps) put you firmly on the road to political stardom. Simply follow these steps, have fun, and good luck!

- **Step 1: Declare your candidacy.** Fill out a statement of eligibility that proves you meet all of the qualifications for state representative. Since you already <u>do</u> meet all of these qualifications, let's move on to the tougher stuff.

- **Step 2: File a personal statement of financial interest.** You must fill out financial disclosure forms that become public record. Basically, these forms reveal a lot about your debts and assets.

- **Step 3: Register with a party.** Or, if you are feeling daring, announce the start of your own party. See the partial list of parties in the section titled "Third Parties" for inspiration.

- **Step 4: Organize a campaign and finance committee.** You will need a lot of helpers with this step. Someone other than you or a family member must administer your campaign and treasury. Your campaign will cost thousands, perhaps even tens of thousands, of dollars.

- **Step 5: Begin campaigning.** Speeches, guest appearances, kissing babies, interviews, etc. Forget about sleep or a private life. You must forsake both of these "luxuries" because name recognition is critical to success. People vote for familiar faces. Remember the incumbent? If this were a horse race, the incumbent would be the favorite, and he would already be three furlongs ahead of you. You, on the other hand, just left the starting gate. Plan on saying many of the same things over and over to dozens of groups.

- **Step 6: Solicit money!** Bags and bags of it. You will need money for television and radio ads and printed materials, such as buttons, posters, and banners, as well as for your political consultants. Staffers should work for free.

- **Step 7: Win or lose.** Step into the voting booth on election day, cross your fingers, and hope that your fellow citizens decided to make you their new state representative!

Name: _____   Date: _____

Campaigns: Kriss Kross

Directions: Use a pencil for this puzzle. Fit the words from the list below in the correct spaces below. There may be two words that fit in the same boxes, but if you are unable to connect the next word, you know you have written in the wrong word. If so, then erase and continue with the other word that does fit.

5 LETTERS	**6 LETTERS**	**8 LETTERS**	**9 LETTERS**	**10 LETTERS**
Plank	Ballot	Campaign	Candidacy	Convention
	Caucus	Ideology		Democratic
	Voters	Platform		Nomination
		Precinct		Republican
				Third Party

11 LETTERS	**12 LETTERS**	**14 LETTERS**	**18 LETTERS**
Split Ticket	Poll Watchers	Political Party	Grassroots Politics
	Polling Place		
	Registration		

The Two-Party System

A **political party** is a group of people organized for the purpose of bringing their issues to the attention of the government and the public. Ours is a two-party system of representation, made up of the Republican and Democratic Parties. Sometimes a third party surfaces to challenge the control of the two major parties. As we see in the section "Third Parties," such groups can make a difference in solving problems untouched by the major parties, such as civil rights, consumer advocacy, and child labor.

The two parties serve a variety of useful functions. They create **platforms** that are statements of the party's basic beliefs. Each part of the platform is known as a **plank**. The Democratic Party, for example, supports unions in its platform. Helping women get the same pay as men for the same labor is a plank of the platform. Another function is the nomination of candidates to fill public office at every level of government from mayor (local) to representative (state) to president (national). These persons are supposed to provide leadership for the citizens who elected them. Political parties form **coalitions** (temporary partnerships) with other interest groups to get popular support for an issue, such as abortion or a Strategic Missile Defense System (SMDS). As part of a successful coalition, a final function of the two parties is achieved—voting. The parties organize and encourage their supporters to show their loyalty and backing of the platform by turning out on **election day** to vote for their candidates.

The Democratic Party dates back to President Andrew Jackson. It is a party that endorses strong, aggressive presidents with followings among citizens of urban areas, unions, and minorities, to name a few. Government, Democrats argue, should play a significant role in helping the nation prosper and achieve social justice. This has traditionally been known as the **liberal** point of view. The Republican Party elected its first president with Abraham Lincoln. It is a party that is backed by business, farmers/rural citizens, and by citizens of suburban areas. Government, according to the Republican Party, should play a limited role in citizens' lives and trust in charity and the goodwill of big business. This is seen as the **conservative** perspective. Both parties, however, try to sit near dead center on the political spectrum because extreme platforms and parties rarely win elections. Thus, for all practical purposes, both parties share similar **ideologies** (philosophies) about preserving the freedoms and rights of citizens.

Another important similarity between the two parties is **organization.** The parties are aligned near the middle of public opinion and support (conservative versus liberal views). This is also known as the "political center." In terms of organization, however, the two parties are very decentralized. As shown in the following breakdown, each party is structured at all levels of government.

The Two-Party System (cont.)

POLITICAL PARTY ORGANIZATION
President
National Party Chairperson
National Committee
National Convention
State Committees
State Caucuses and Conventions
County, City, and Town Committees
Ward and Precinct Organizations
Precinct Captains
Voters

These levels of organization may seem mysterious to some; however, a brief word of explanation may help sort out the confusion. Both parties use the above pyramidal structure. A **convention** is an official meeting or gathering of a political party. Its basic purpose is to select its primary candidates for national and state elections, announce the party platform, and assess the party's prospects for success in the upcoming election(s). A Democrat, for instance, running for office in a suburban area that is overwhelmingly Republican will not win. Few party resources will be allocated to help a candidate in a losing cause.

The **caucus** is an enigma (mystery) to many voters. It is an assembly of politicians who craft policies and try to nominate candidates for their party. What truly makes this process different from a convention is that these decisions occur behind closed doors (out of public view). We do not know how effective or powerful such meetings are in contemporary politics.

A **precinct**, on the other hand, is a local voting district found in cities, counties, and wards. Leaders of the precinct are known as **captains**. Typically, the captains use committees to nominate candidates and organize voters to help the political party. This is called **grassroots politics**, the level at which the average voter can participate directly in party business by being a volunteer, voting for the **party slate** (list of candidates), donating money and resources, and running for public office. For someone interested in politics, the precinct is the first stepping stone.

Third Parties

"The more you read and observe about this Politics thing, you got to admit that each party is worse than the other. The one that's out always looks the best."

—Will Rogers

There is a long tradition of minor or **third party** movements in our political history. Sometimes these parties may build a **constituency** (following) based on only one or two issues or on nothing more than a candidate's charisma! Such parties often have a short life span as enthusiasm for their agenda wanes. They have achieved some success in areas such as child labor, consumer rights, women's suffrage, and environmentalism. Third parties act as outlets or alternatives for voters who feel that the Democratic and Republican parties have failed them. Members of third parties, in other words, do not believe that the two-party system truly represents their interests. ("Nobody listens to me in government!") These people look to third parties for help. No third-party candidate, however, has ever won the presidency. However, this has not discouraged many types of groups from organizing into political third parties. As you will see below, a wide range of interests is promoted in these splinter groups.

Guide to Third Parties in American Politics

Name	Descriptors
AP = American Party	Small, ultra-conservative Christian group
AHP = American Heritage Party	Uses the Bible as a political textbook for running a national and/or state government
ANP = American Nazi Party	Pro-White racists
FVP = Family Values Party	Exactly what the title implies
GP = Grassroots Party	Pro-marijuana, environment, and universal healthcare
GPUS = Green Party U.S.	Left-wing environmental reformist group
IP = Independence Party	Governor Jesse Ventura's populist group
LP = Libertarian Party	Advocates complete personal freedoms
PP = Prohibition Party	Anti-Communist and anti-drug
LP = Light Party	Bizarre mix of holistic, New Age politics
RP = Reform Party	Billionaire Ross Perot's party of conservatives
SP = Southern Party	Wants the South to re-fight the Civil War
PP = Pot Party	Exactly what the title implies

Name: _____ Date: _____

Rally Around the Cause!

Here is your chance to try something that most people will never experience—to form a political party. This is a hypothetical situation (for now), in which you and your classmates try to build a workable, functioning political party. Answer each of the questions as simply and directly as possible. At the conclusion of the question/answer set, present your new political party to your classmates and watch their reactions. [**Hint:** Do not try to appeal to everyone in your **party platform** (statement of beliefs and values).]

1. What is the name of your party? _____

2. What is your party symbol (e.g., donkey, elephant, etc.)? _____

3. What is your party motto? _____

_____

4. What are four "things you stand for" (e.g., pro-life, etc.) in your party?

   • _____

   • _____

   • _____

   • _____

5. What groups or types of people would be attracted to your party? Why?

_____

_____

_____

6. How would you attract public support and media attention?

_____

_____

_____

7. What obstacles do you expect to meet in the promotion of your new party?

_____

_____

8. How would you successfully sponsor one of your candidates for public office?

_____

_____

_____

Name: _____ Date: _____

Political Parties: Word Search

Directions: Find and circle the words listed below in the word search puzzle. Words may be printed forward, backward, up, down, or diagonally.

```
X O I L G Z H V P A V O U X D B M X R M I L P G
J Q C S W K N A C I L B U P E R H B U K F W L S
A K U I U V Q I H A S M X J C R S C W Q J U Q P
N X J J I C I D A S T T M C F O V T V P Q S X T
O Q C R X K U K D L U U C O N V E N T I O N G W
I X G N X Z I A H A Z V V D V U G D H F N S F O
T P R C E S K D C T D F C E L E C T I O N N S P
A G E P I J V G D E L C F Y W Q R Y G T E Z K A
N U F N H H R O C F N V V K A X K V W T S N E R
I C O H L F P V U F V P E X R G M F K Y Q Y Y T
M M R Z Z I N T W Q S A I E T A D I D N A C H Y
O N M F V G B W X O P W P C Q V K Q K A B V P S
N D P D D Y Y E E C K Y F M X V D G P Y F W Y Y
A M A L R B K M R P L A T F O R M M C L S T D S
S D R C W S Q Y W T K K K U M I Y P X F R L X T
C H T X F W R Z A W A U S M G U Q Y H A T L K E
G R Y W K H C I Y M X R M P X F K G P H A T R M
G G B I Z E K W N X B I I G M U C D P W R O V W
U F J B T N N C Z W M L Z A G H R O W Y C X H R
M M Z Z P Y A Z D J C R S X N I K Z H G O Y J D
T D B L G H L B D S V K A K H X N G H A M E A J
D E R O C X P P H U M C T T Z K P K N M E D H X
T L J P U N Y C C W M E T D W P G F D K D S P F
W A R G R A S S R O O T S R I P E U W J X D S S
```

WORD LIST

Candidate	Caucus	Convention	Democrat
Election	Grassroots	Libertarian	Nomination
Plank	Platform	Reform Party	Republican
Slate	Third Party	Two-Party System	

31

The Legislative Branch: Congress

The United States Congress makes laws. It contains two branches or "houses." The House of Representatives has 435 members that come from the districts within their respective states. Each district should be roughly equal in population (not geographic size), and each member of the House represents about 500,000 to 600,000 citizens. Current information from the census is used to properly redistribute seats in the House. This is also referred to as **reapportionment**. The controversial process of **gerrymandering** has often been used to redraw district lines to give an "edge" to a political party or to minimize the political strength of another group. Hence, it matters a great deal to know the population of each state in order to decipher who gains or

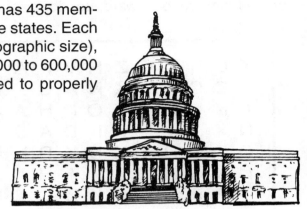

loses seats in the House of Representatives. The Senate has only 100 members, two per state. Senators serve for a six-year term, whereas Representatives run for reelection every two years. However, the terms for Senators are on a staggered schedule, so one-third of the Senate is up for reelection every two years as well. On the first Tuesday after the first Monday in November (even-numbered years), elections are conducted throughout the country for both houses of Congress. Congress is an elected assembly, but it does not reflect the **electorate** (voting body). Most members of Congress are White males from high-income families, with above-average education backgrounds, and a disproportionate number are from the "professional class," especially lawyers and businesspersons.

On the third day of January at noon, the houses of **Congress** (House and Senate) meet in their respective chambers and start a **session** (term of work). Normally, Congress is in session from January until fall, with numerous breaks for vacations and campaigning. A typical work week for both houses is about four days, Monday through Thursday. The House membership is presided over by a **Speaker**. The Speaker is the leader of the party that has the largest number of members in the House of Representatives. The Speaker "keeps legislative business moving" and casts the tie-breaking vote when necessary. The Vice President of the United States is the official Senate president. However, a president **pro tempore** (temporary) usually presides over the Senate. This person is often from the majority party or may be selected on a rotating basis.

Virtually all of the work of Congress pivots around the system of **committees** and subcommittees in both Houses. Whenever any **bill** is presented for consideration, it is automatically sent to a committee. From there the bill takes one or more routes, which include: full hearings before a committee; the referral of the bill to a subcommittee; or the bill is **killed** (ignored). If the bill is debated, it is placed on a **calendar**, and both sides have a stake in the outcome. Opponents may use rules and stall tactics to stop a proposed bill from reaching the House floor for a vote. In the Senate, opponents may also resort to a **filibuster**, a nonstop speech that obstructs any other discussion of a bill under review. At some point, every bill reaches some sort of outcome either as a new law, a defeated proposal, or a **tabled** (put aside) issue. The same issue/bill may be resurrected at any session of Congress for review and debate.

The Legislative Branch: Congress (cont.)

The powers of the Congress are closely linked to its legislative functions or goals. Some of its most critical powers include:

- Collecting/raising taxes and borrowing/making money. This money, in turn, is earmarked for expenses in "running the country" (e.g., Social Security, crime control, etc.).
- Declaring war and making peace.
- Providing for the national defense by maintaining armed forces.
- The regulation of interstate and international trade/industry/business.
- The authority to admit new states.
- Creating and maintaining the federal court system.
- Administering the postal services.
- The responsibility for setting uniform standards of weights and measures.
- Granting copyrights and patents.
- Maintaining a national highway system.
- The power of impeachment when a federal official (from judges to presidents) is accused of a serious crime or **treason** (the betrayal of one's nation).

At the same time, Congress cannot exceed its lawful authority by, among other things, passing laws that convict persons without trial (**bill of attainde**r). Other restrictions on Congress's powers are bans on passing any laws that "break" the spirit of the Bill of Rights or laws that take effect after something has happened (**ex post facto laws**). We do not want, for instance, Congress to have the authority to pass a law that punishes an unpopular person or group. The Supreme Court is an important tool in repealing unlawful or unconstitutional acts by Congress. Needless to say, such attempts by Congress to "redefine" the Constitution are typically challenged by interest groups through the courts.

"Laws, like houses, lean on one another." —Edmund Burke, 1765

Did You Know That ...

 Representatives and senators receive an annual salary of $145,000 plus LOTS of "perks" and benefits, such as free mail, free trips, a suite of offices with staff, and expense accounts? As the saying goes—"Nice work if you can get it!"

Name: _____   Date: _____

The Legislative Branch: Word Search

Directions: Find and circle the words listed below in the word search puzzle. Words may be printed forward, backward, up, down, or diagonally.

```
V R W I  B X S B X F A L B C F E Z C C F S M J U
E S D R S H U I  I  Y F Y Z A M H H E V N U E C S
S G F C E V O L M I  T Z W N S G Y G Q K N T B C
S E Q R P E I  L Z A B E J H Z Y P G E C N H Q I
U L N A O B G A C E V I  T A T N E S E R P E R T
N S E A U I  S G K C Y A E K P J Z B W H O V U I
E H X S T K Q Y C L Y X L X H F R P A W F P U L
Y A T C R O G C J G M L G X Z T Y Y P R P W K O
Q E A O N G R F U F N R X B A Z T T R O W M B P
R F M U G Y I  Z A U W I  S U D M H L R O G S Z D
M T K D D R I  D E R X S K I  Y Q U K D Q P Q I  O
O N Z T O T Z F J Q M P C A U F B V M V C L N P
B W Q C E E T T I  M M O C I  M A O Z R W L O V M
S U J H J Z C H T G B K F B R W Z C M U E B E C
X C Q A W O Y T Y M M J E R U E A Y F H Q B F C
D M S I  V K M F T N E L E B W U M L V D E Y E J
G Z Z R S N N W A S Q L E R C N F R W Q I  I  M E
Z T A M X M X D E Y D Z F G D G K U P A J S J T
N Q L A Q U W T S F I  N C U M B E N T E H T F A
Q W S N B F B T E E Y Z N H C G A S C J I  R B Y
K X E I  A W F K F Z Y C F U H V V U G Y Q V I  N
E D J B K Y N B A O I  C B E F U O Q J Z L P D G
A Z D L V I  T S S E W F U N Z N G M P D W S M A
T G O S S E R G N O C I  N T E R E S T G R O U P
```

WORD LIST

Bill	Chairman	Committee	Congress	Filibuster
Incumbent	Interest Group	Lawmaking	Lobbyist	Politics
Pork Barrel	Representative	Rider	Safe Seat	Senator

34

From an Idea to a Law

Any citizen may write a **bill** in the hope of making it into a law. Every law begins with an idea. Once written, the idea becomes a bill that must be sponsored by a legislator. The legislator then introduces the bill, which is assigned a number and letter (e.g., H.R.100 [House] or S.100 [Senate]). From there, the bill is sent to a committee and printed. At that point, the legislative or lawmaking process begins with the following stages:

Stage 1:   **Referred to the committee** (depending on the type of subject, e.g., energy conservation, commerce, etc.)

Stage 2:   **Action by the committee** (e.g., placed on a calendar and reviewed)

Stage 3:   **Subcommittee Review** (e.g., hearings and further study)

Stage 4:   **Mark-up** (changes to the bill)

Stage 5:   **Committee action to report a bill** (The committee votes on its changes to the House or Senate.)

Stage 6:   **Publication of a report** (with summary remarks that explain the scope, effect, and impact of the legislation)

Stage 7:   **Floor action scheduled** (The proposed bill is placed on the legislative calendar.)

Stage 8:   **Debate on the proposed bill**

Stage 9:   **Voting for or against the proposed bill**

Stage 10:   **Referral to the House or Senate** (depending on where the bill originated)

Stage 11:   **Conference committee action** (requires approval of both houses)

Stage 12:   **Final action** (The bill signed by the House and Senate is sent to the president for approval. He may sign or veto the bill.)

Stage 13:   **Veto override** (A two-thirds vote of Congress is needed to override a presidential veto.)

As you can see, it is a lengthy, time-consuming process that rewards the determination of the sponsor(s). If, after these 13 stages are completed, a bill "survives" the gauntlet of reviews and debates, the idea then becomes a law of the land.

Mock Congress: "Build Your Own Law"

Pretend that you and your classmates are United States senators, each from a different state. Pick a state, a political party, and an **ideology** (political beliefs). Ideally, there should be an equal number of Democrats and Republicans in the exercise. A very controversial issue has been brought to your attention by the press, and public opinion is starting to build throughout the country. Action is called for by your constituents. In short—do something!

THE ISSUE:

"Should women be allowed to fight in frontline combat in all branches of the armed forces?"

This exercise is a three-step process. First, take a **stand** on the issue (debate and persuasion). Second, write a short and simple law that either forbids or allows women to serve as combat personnel in the military. (Be very careful of your wording!) This law, by the way, can also be rewritten and altered by other classmates. The third and final step is—VOTE!

Listen to your classmates. Everyone is entitled to his or her own point of view, even if you disagree with that person. Remember also that your own values and judgments may not reflect your state or voters on this issue. A mistake on this volatile topic could cost you a lot of voter support at the next election. As a starting point, therefore, try answering the following questions:

- What is my position on women in combat? For example, are women as capable as men in battle?
- What are my chances of success or failure with this law?
- Who is with or against me on this legislation?
- How can I maneuver others to vote with me in passing this law?
- What will be my central arguments during the debates?

At the conclusion of a prearranged time block, a vote should be held with each senator announcing his/her decision aloud to the group. Tally the votes, and announce the winning side. Afterwards, discuss briefly some of the difficulties that you encountered in tackling this issue. For example, was it easy or difficult to build a coalition of classmates who shared your views? What would you do differently on future topics? Finally, what insights did you gain about the nature of the legislative process?

The House of Representatives

If you are at least 25 years of age, a resident of the state, and an American citizen for seven years, you may run for election to the U.S. House of Representatives. The "House" has 435 members; the number of representatives is keyed to the size of a state's population (and the district you live in). States with small populations, for example, like North Dakota and South Dakota, qualify for only one representative apiece. You will run for office during each even-numbered year for a two-year term of office. A **HUGE** factor in figuring out your chances of success is this: **incumbents** (those already in office) will win approximately 90 percent of their bids for reelection. This means that unless you are wealthy and have realistic expectations for victory, virtually few (about 10 percent) of the <u>new</u> candidates for the House of Representatives will defeat the incumbents.

If you do win, however, the question becomes "what happens now?"! The House is large, complex, full of rules, and run through an elaborate network of **committees.** There are approximately 22 standing committees and roughly 130 subcommittees. Members serve on many committees, depending on their seniority and power. Newly-elected members will not be appointed to important posts on the major committees. Three committees, in fact, are seen as the most influential in the House: Rules, Appropriations, and Ways and Means. The Committee on Rules supervises how things get done in the House. The Appropriations Committee administers all money bills that fund government functions and agencies. Lastly, the Ways and Means committee deals with tax issues and proposals. Proposed tax bills or measures start in the House. Some observers have noted that the primary duty of the House seems to be the care of money—spending, raising, and minting! No proposed bill can really expect to get passed without successfully negotiating the intense review of these three committees. The House, therefore, is a very busy place to work; an estimated 9,000 to 12,000 bills are considered and processed annually.

The House is more closely tied to the voters because each member is up for reelection every two years. Representatives must be active both in Congress and in their home districts. The House, therefore, is described as a "democratic" institution whose members more accurately reflect the **electorate** (voters). It is the House of Representatives, for instance, that possesses the formal power of **impeachment** or the removal of government officials (e.g., federal judges and presidents). Also, if the Electoral College does not issue a majority vote for a single candidate for president (a very rare event), then the House elects a president. Each state receives one vote to cast. Clearly, the House of Representatives has many functions, responsibilities, and powers that enable it to wield a great deal of influence over the legislative process.

The Senate

To be eligible to become a U.S. Senator, one must be a citizen of the country for nine years, a state resident, and at least 30 years old. The **Senate** is an exclusive body of members; only two per state, for a total of 100 senators—state size does not matter. Every state sends two senators to Washington, D.C., for a six-year term. In every even-numbered year, one third of the Senate seats are up for election. Like the House of Representatives, incumbents usually win most of the time. Unless a candidate is a White male, wealthy, and from the upper social/professional classes, the chances of victory are marginal.

Did You Know That ...

 In 1992, Carol Mosely Braun was the first African-American female to be elected to the Senate?

Even though the Senate has far fewer members than the House, it handles a large workload. Every year it processes anywhere from 9,500 to 12,000 bills, plus many public/private laws; it is a complex institution. Detailed rules, 44 to be exact, numerous committees, and large staffs run the Senate. All senators are expected to serve on several committees and subcommittees. Staffers help operate the committee calendars and do much of the research needed to understand the issues brought before the Senate. To keep business moving, both political parties in the Senate unanimously consent to agreements. A unique rule of this body is that of **cloture of debate.** This refers to a three-fifths vote of the Senate to close or end debate and proceed with a vote on a bill. This is a much-needed rule because the Senate permits unlimited debate. A handful of senators can block further action on a bill by invoking the tradition of unrestricted debate. The cloture rule overcomes that obstacle to progress.

The Senate is an extremely powerful lawmaking assembly. It shares many legislative functions and duties with the House of Representatives, but it has three exclusive Constitutional powers. First, the Senate **ratifies** (by two-thirds vote) all treaties the president enters into with foreign governments. Second, it must **confirm** (by majority vote) presidential nominations (e.g., Supreme Court, Cabinet appointments, etc.). Last, the Senate acts as a court or tribunal in cases of impeachment (by two-thirds vote) sent to it from the House. To date, only four federal officials (all judges) have ever been removed from office through impeachment. The Senate is seen as a somewhat independent branch of government. Certainly, its six-year term is significant—senators are supposed to represent the "big picture" of American policy and lawmaking by not having to worry about frequent elections. Job security, in other words, is a key ingredient in Senate life. It is the closest thing we have to an aristocracy in American government.

Name: _____ Date: _____

Congress: Kriss Kross

Directions: Use a pencil for this puzzle. Fit the words from the list below in the correct spaces below. There may be two words that fit in the same boxes, but if you are unable to connect the next word, you know you have written in the wrong word. If so, then erase and continue with the other word that does fit.

3 LETTERS	**4 LETTERS**	**6 LETTERS**	**7 LETTERS**	**8 LETTERS**
Law	Bill	Tabled	Senator	Calendar
	Term		Session	
			Speaker	

9 LETTERS	**10 LETTERS**	**11 LETTERS**	**14 LETTERS**	**15 LETTERS**
Committee	Electorate	Ex Post Facto	Gerrymandering	Bill of Attainder
Incumbent	Filibuster	Impeachment	Representative	Cloture of Debate
	Pro Tempore			Reapportionment

The Judicial Branch: The Courts

The **judicial branch** interprets federal laws, treaties, and the Constitution. It consists of the Supreme Court, the United States Federal District Courts, special courts, and the United States Courts of Appeal. Each court has a **jurisdiction**. Jurisdiction refers to the specific authority or right of a court to hear and review a case. It is a complex idea. There are different types of jurisdiction. Some courts have jurisdiction over certain <u>types</u> of cases or according to the <u>location</u> of cases. (e.g., a city speeding ticket violation would not be heard in federal district court.) Also, there are classifications of federal and state courts based on **original, appellate, exclusive,** and **concurrent** jurisdiction. These ideas are defined later. For now, keep in mind that the federal courts can preside over cases (jurisdiction) in which:

- Someone is charged with violating the Constitution or a treaty.
- Citizens from different states have a lawsuit.
- A crime occurs at sea on an American ship.
- A person is charged with breaking a federal law.
- A foreign nation decides to sue the government or a citizen of the United States.
- States have a conflict or lawsuit, or
- A crime is committed on federal property (e.g., park lands, military bases, etc.).

A federal court that is the first to hear a case has **original jurisdiction**. Courts that review the decisions of lower federal courts have **appellate jurisdiction**. Some federal courts, like the Supreme Court, have both types of jurisdiction. **Concurrent jurisdiction** means that the federal and state courts share authority over a case. A bank robber or white-collar offender, for example, could be tried in both the federal and state courts. **Exclusive jurisdiction** is the right of the federal courts to solely preside over specific types of cases (e.g., a music copyright). No local or state court has the authority to hear the case.

This notion that the federal courts may review and possibly overturn the decisions of other government branches is known as **judicial review**. This power was established in *Marbury v. Madison* (1803) when the Supreme Court declared that the courts must have the freedom to act as a check on the legislative and executive branches. The Supreme Court went even further in *McCulloch v. Maryland* (1819) by stating that federal law was supreme. Furthermore, the national government had **implied powers**, or powers that are not specifically laid out in the Constitution but still exist in order to administer the country (e.g., creating federal banks). Thus, the Supreme Court announced in two landmark decisions that: (1) the federal courts must be empowered to overturn the laws of Congress that were unconstitutional; and (2) the laws of the federal government were supreme, unless reversed by the Supreme Court.

The Judicial Branch: The Courts (cont.)

Unlike the state court systems, federal courts exist in a unified system. Their center of power is the Constitution, laws, rules, and regulations. The federal system of courts is simply organized, as you will see below.

FEDERAL COURT SYSTEM

Level 1: Supreme Court of the United States

Level 2: U.S. Courts of Appeal (13 circuits, six or more judges per court)
- Hears appeals from criminal/civil courts, such as Federal District Courts, U.S. Claims Court, and U.S. Court of Military Appeals

Level 3: Federal District Courts (94 courts)
- Federal trial courts (original jurisdiction) for criminal/civil cases

This is a straightforward approach to judicial organization. The country is divided into 13 judicial circuits. A **circuit** is a broad geographic region, which includes a number of federal courts. A **district** is a sub-unit or area within the circuit.

Every federal court is run by a federal judge. All federal judges are appointed by the president. Their terms of office are for life—they keep the job for as long as they wish or until they are removed by impeachment. Federal judges share many similar traits. They are generally middle-aged, White, male Protestants who graduated from prestigious law schools. They are usually successful lawyers or judges, affluent, and from the same political party as the president. It is only in the last ten to 15 years that minorities and women have occasionally been appointed to a federal judgeship. For the most part, a federal judge shares the president's values and philosophies. The president appoints a candidate to the federal court in the hope that he or she will support and extend his policies and programs through favorable bench decisions. Once promoted to the bench after senatorial approval, a federal judge is relatively immune from outside "tampering" or interference from the other two branches of government. Of these various appointments, however, none are subjected to as much careful scrutiny as those involving the United States **Supreme Court**.

The Supreme Court

Nine people sit on the U.S. Supreme Court, a chief justice and eight associate justices. Each is appointed by the president. The Supreme Court decides the constitutionality of federal laws and presidential decisions. As people, groups, and agencies send their requests to have an appeal review, the court must decide which cases to consider. Four justices must agree to a hearing. This is called the **Rule of Four**. If this occurs, a **writ of certiorari** is issued. The writ is an order to the lower court to forward the **transcripts** (records) of the case. Although the Supreme Court receives so many requests annually (over 5,000), it can only review a small number of cases (approximately 150 to 200) each year.

As a result, the Supreme Court must issue writs of certiorari carefully and on the basis of merit. There are several reasons for denying a petition or request for review. A person, for instance, who was not harmed by a law that he/she challenged will not have the case heard. Another example involves **moot issues**; the court will not review an issue or question that makes no difference or has already been settled elsewhere. Sometimes the court will reject a petition because it thinks the issue should be settled by the executive or legislative branches. Technically speaking, **ALL** citizens have the right to petition the Supreme Court. This does not mean that the court is under any obligation to hear the request. The poorest citizen can file a **brief** at no cost through a document known as the "Pauper's Petition." A brief is simply a document that describes a person's side of the case or legal issue in question. A lawyer may be appointed free of charge by the court to represent the poor petitioner.

After both sides in a case file their briefs, the justices convene to hold oral arguments in open court. Each lawyer is allocated about 30 minutes to argue his/her side with interruptions for questions by the justices. Thereafter, the justices meet to discuss the briefs, oral arguments, and each other's viewpoints or positions. Then, a vote is taken. A majority (six justices form a quorum) is needed to reach a decision. Written opinions by the majority and the views of members of the minority are drafted and circulated for comments. One justice is selected to write the final majority opinion for public viewing. Dissenting views of other justices are included in the opinion.

It is very helpful to note that court decisions follow the principle of **stare decisis** or precedent. That is, the court will abide by previous decisions on an issue unless an urgent reason exists to depart from the past. If the court breaks with precedent, such decisions are often tagged as **landmark cases**; they announce a new direction for the court. These are often controversial and ignite nationwide debate as in the areas of civil rights, abortion, obscenity, the separation of church and state, and gun ownership. As you might suppose, the Supreme Court is very reluctant to tackle cases that might propel them into the arena of public criticism. By making a highly unpopular decision, the Court risks losing popular support for its authority.

Name: _____ Date: _____

The Judicial Branch: Word Search

Directions: Find and circle the words listed below in the word search puzzle. Words may be printed forward, backward, up, down, or diagonally.

```
F R U L E O F F O U R L R W H E G A P K A L I Z
A O W N I Y V M C K W V G I X X D D J V J V K C
P U P B V K C T V W I K C T M T T G A J K D I M
P S B H D B J H M A R B U R Y V M A D I S O N B
O A V C G B F W J Z L W D L R Q M U H E F I G R
I K U H L A Y E G V J K J H L F F C M C I E E B
N Q Y R G W A I M M L L V O K O O H A X Y S R Y
T Q V H S L Y V X I N D E D L B N I M P U I N G
M Q V S T G W E N N I O F F Y Q Y E Q Q E U R A
E F V E G W Q R M R Q N I Z X W K F S F G A H Q
N O U G A W S L Z N B R U N Z D N J N O C P H V
T T D D H T G A F Z D C H G I B C U M I B D B K
G E W U C Y B I B U Z I A I T P K S O T W S B T
H T R J I R V C Z L B A B N E K O T J R G H W Z
X Z Q B S K O I O A G E E A A A U I W U Z R H F
U S T A T E Y D V R F V A X K Y L C Y O C U D Z
I G P V Q P T U Z E K F S J O F S E F C O Q E O
R K D B B H I J C D E O C M I X I K D E R H C N
I S O Q V U E U J E F C O P Y A M A F M F Z I Z
G M C W E J I U E F H D R G I N Y L T E K H S O
T S K Z U I G S F I S E P L O S W K K R W L I X
E Y E Q Z F R Z C R Y N U U S N R K J P G L O T
S Z T B B B Q X W R I T U S I J T W P P U S T N R
S J T V U S N U X H C K Z K J B J B N S N U Q Q
```

WORD LIST

Appointment	Brief	Chief Justice	Decision
Docket	Federal	Habeas Corpus	Judges
Judicial Review	Marbury v. Madison	Opinion	Rule of Four
State	Supreme Court	Writ	

43

Name: _____ Date: _____

The Federal Court System: Kriss Kross

Directions: Use a pencil for this puzzle. Fit the words from the list below in the correct spaces below. There may be two words that fit in the same boxes, but if you are unable to connect the next word, you know you have written in the wrong word. If so, then erase and continue with the other word that does fit.

J U D I C I A L R E V I E W

5 LETTERS	**7 LETTERS**	**8 LETTERS**	**9 LETTERS**	**10 LETTERS**
Brief	Circuit	District	Appellate	Concurrent
	Marbury	Justices	Exclusive	Moot Issues
		Opinions		Rule of Four
		Original		

11 LETTERS	**12 LETTERS**	**13 LETTERS**	**14 LETTERS**	**16 LETTERS**
Transcripts	Jurisdiction	Federal Courts	Judicial Review	Writ of Certiorari
	Stare Decisis	Landmark Cases		
	Supreme Court			

The Executive Branch: The Presidency

"All the President is, is a glorified public relations man who spends his time flattering, kissing, kicking people to get them to do what they are supposed to do anyway." —Harry S Truman, 1947

The **executive branch** of government is chartered to carry out and execute federal laws. It consists of: the offices of the president and vice president, 15 federal departments, various agencies, the Federal Reserve System, the White House office, boards/commissions/committees, and the Cabinet. It is the president's task to administer and manage the affairs of the executive branch.

To become president, a person must be at least 35 years old, a "natural-born" citizen, and reside within the country for at least 14 years. Since the time of George Washington, presidents have generally shared most of the following unofficial "requirements" before assuming office. Most presidents have been White males, Protestant, born to affluent families, married, reared in rural areas, college graduates, and from military backgrounds. These characteristics have changed little over time.

The job of president is extremely complex. The duties and responsibilities are numerous and far-reaching. As compensation to offset the stress and demands of the job, there are many attractive "perks" or benefits attached to the position. These include:

- Residency in the White House, complete with a private theater, pool, library, gymnasium, conference rooms, dining rooms, and a bowling alley;
- Annual salary of $340,000;
- Access to Camp David, a sprawling vacation resort;
- A nontaxable travel account;
- Annual expense account of $50,000;
- White House staff, complete with chefs, butlers, maids, and groundskeepers;
- Personal on-call staff of healthcare professionals;
- Unlimited use of Air Force One, jets, and helicopters;
- First-class accommodations anywhere in the United States;
- Secret Service protection (including that of family members); and
- Outstanding retirement benefits package.

Should a president need to be replaced due to death or removal from office, an **order of succession** has been developed. Eleven public officials stand in line to assume the job and functions of the office of president. The first six, in priority, are the vice president, the Speaker of the House, the president pro tempore of the Senate, the secretary of state, the secretary of the treasury, and the attorney general.

The Executive Branch: The Presidency (cont.)

The obligations and powers of the president, as noted earlier, are impressive. He is involved in matters that pertain to all branches of the federal government. He serves as a spokesperson, symbol, leader, and decision-maker for the nation. Public attention and opinion tend to focus on the statements and decisions of the president, rather than that of Congress or the judicial branch. The office of president is far more visible to the media and the public eye. To perform his duties effectively, the president relies on astute advisors within the various organizations of the executive branch. One example of this reliance is the Cabinet, which includes the chiefs of all 15 executive departments. Usually, the vice president is also included in Cabinet meetings. Additional agencies and heads have Cabinet rank membership, such as the Office of Management and Budget and the Environmental Protection Agency. These executives offer advice and information to the president on those topics relating to their areas of expertise.

What then are the general powers of the president? Review the list below. Try to identify for each power what areas of government, issues, or people would be most affected by the president's authority.

The general powers of the president are to:

- Propose legislation to Congress.
- Appoint federal officials; this power needs a majority vote of approval by the U.S. Senate in its role of offering "advice and consent."
- Enforce federal laws; one tool for accomplishing this goal is the **executive order**. An executive order is a rule or command issued by the president in order to enforce a law or treaty.
- Serve as commander in chief of the armed forces.
- **Veto**; a president may block legislation by vetoing (forbidding) its passage. It is interesting to note that Congress has historically overridden very few vetoes.
- Use the power of **executive privilege/immunity**. This is also known as the limited right of presidents to withhold information from Congress and/or the courts.
- Issue **reprieves** (postpone a punishment), **pardons** (release from a punishment), and **amnesty** (general pardon for a group of people).
- Make **treaties** with other foreign governments (with the approval of the Senate).
- Maintain emergency funding (e.g., disasters).
- Use the prerogative of **executive agreement**. This is an agreement or understanding between the president and the leader of a foreign government. It does not require formal approval by the Senate.
- Appoint diplomats.

It is no wonder, therefore, that a president is under constant public scrutiny for his decisions. These decisions may have a profound effect on the nation's economy, national defense, general welfare, and prosperity. The eyes of the nation and the world are always attuned to the Oval Office at 1600 Pennsylvania Avenue.

Name: _____   Date: _____

The Executive Branch: Kriss Kross

Directions: Use a pencil for this puzzle. Fit the words from the list below in the correct spaces below. There may be two words that fit in the same boxes, but if you are unable to connect the next word, you know you have written in the wrong word. If so, then erase and continue with the other word that does fit.

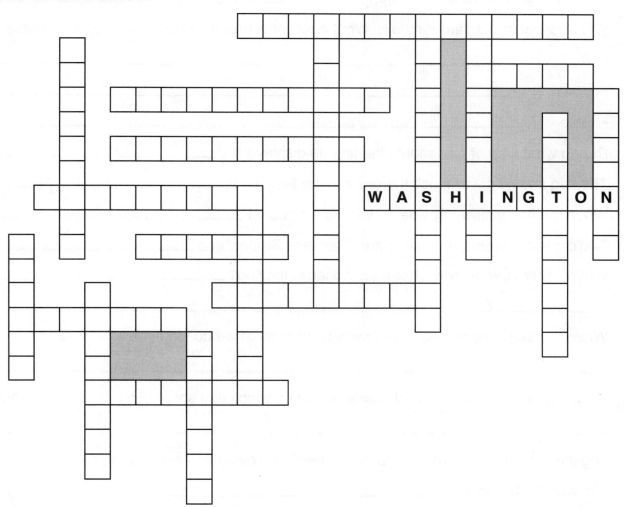

5 LETTERS	**6 LETTERS**	**7 LETTERS**	**8 LETTERS**	**9 LETTERS**
Adams	Pardon	Amnesty	Immunity	Jefferson
	Treaty	Cabinet	Reprieve	Roosevelt
		Lincoln		Veto Power
				War Powers

10 LETTERS	**11 LETTERS**	**12 LETTERS**	**13 LETTERS**	**14 LETTERS**
Oval Office	Impeachment	Chief of State	Vice President	Executive Order
Succession				
Washington				
White House				

The American Flag: Vital Facts

Directions: Read the series of important questions below about the American flag. Then test your practical knowledge about the flag by trying to correctly answer the questions. Good luck!

1. What do the 13 stripes on the flag represent? _____

2. The colors of the flag are symbolic. What ideals or virtues do each of these colors represent?

    • Red   = _____

    • White = _____

    • Blue   = _____

3. During what time of day should the flag be displayed? _____

4. The flag should never touch the ground, the floor, or _____.

5. When the flag is flown upside down, it is a signal of _____.

6. Two common names for the flag are "Stars and Stripes" and _____.

7. Why, over time, were new white stars added to the flag? _____

    _____

8. When the flag is being raised or lowered, what must we do to salute it?

    _____

9. If a group of national flags is clustered together, which flag should be raised the highest?

    _____

10. Legend says that this woman was responsible for designing and sewing the first American flag. Who was she? _____

11. What was the phrase, "Don't Tread on Me"?

    _____

    _____

12. If the flag is flown at night, it must always be _____.

13. What famous song, written by Francis Scott Key in 1814, was inspired by the American flag? _____

The Executive Departments

Fourteen executive departments exist in the national government. The president is responsible for supervising the operations of these agencies. Each department has a general area of interest. In a nutshell, the general duties of each department can be stated as follows:

1. **Department of Veterans Affairs:** Provides services and program aid to veterans and their families, including hospital care, education benefits, pensions, and home loans.

2. **Department of Labor:** Oversees labor standards, practices, and employment services.

3. **Department of State:** Issues passports/visas and attends to matters dealing with foreign relations/issues.

4. **Department of Transportation:** Supervises national transportation safety, policy, and federal aid to states for highways.

5. **Department of the Treasury:** Makes currency and collects taxes for the government.

6. **Department of Energy:** Determines national policies for energy, conservation, and regulation of power supplies.

7. **Department of Agriculture:** Handles matters of interest to farmers (e.g., crop markets), inspects meat products, and regulates school lunch and food stamp programs.

8. **Department of Justice:** Investigates and prosecutes violators of federal law(s) and administers immigration and naturalization policies.

9. **Department of Defense:** Manages all branches of the armed forces and military bases for the nation.

10. **Department of the Interior:** Supervises federal parks/lands and Indian reservations.

11. **Department of Health and Human Services:** Oversees Social Security, public health programs, and monitors safe foods/medicines.

12. **Department of Education:** Administers education programs, dispenses federal aid, and conducts research.

13. **Department of Commerce:** Responsible for regulation of trade, business, and weights and measures.

14. **Department of Housing and Urban Development (HUD):** Responsible for aiding in city housing, mass transit, and traffic issues.

15. **Department of Homeland Security:** Responsible for developing and coordinating a comprehensive national strategy to strengthen protections against terrorist threats or attacks in the United States.

Name: _____   Date: _____

The Executive Departments: Word Scrambler

Directions: Unscramble the words below using the words in the word bank.

Agriculture	**Armed Forces**	**Commerce**	**Defense**
Departments	**Education**	**Energy**	**Executive Branch**
Health	**Homeland Security**	**Housing**	**Human Services**
Interior	**Justice**	**Labor**	**State**
Transportation	**Treasury**	**Urban Development**	

1. DEIACUTON _____

2. STAET _____

3. CERMEMCO _____

4. SNEARTEV FSAARIF _____

5. SUTCJEI _____

6. BAUNR VEPETNOLEDM _____

7. RELUTCAUGIR _____

8. REASTUYR _____

9. EDESNEF _____

10. IENRITRO _____

11. ATHLEH _____

12. EYRGNE _____

13. ALROB _____

14. AITTAONRTPRNOS _____

15. EMADR FSCROE _____

16. ITUVEEXCE RCBHAN _____

17. NHUAM VECIRESS _____

18. TMNETAPREDS _____

19. UISGHON _____

20. ENHOADLM CIYTUSER _____

The Pentagon: A City Unto Itself

The Pentagon is a huge five-sided structure that is often referred to as a "city unto itself" because it resembles a modern city in form and function. The Department of Defense (DOD) is housed in the Pentagon. The **Joint Chiefs of Staff**, part of DOD, work at the Pentagon. Each branch of the armed services—army, navy, air force, and marines—is represented in the Joint Chiefs of Staff with the fifth member chosen as Chairman by the president. Their responsibilities are critical to the safety of the country. This group oversees the nation's military, including bases, and advises the president on all matters pertaining to the armed services. Their work, to say the least, requires a great deal of room.

Completed in 1943, the Pentagon is rated as one of the largest office buildings in the world with over 3.7 million square feet of floor space. It is also considered to be one of the most efficiently designed facilities ever built. Even though the Pentagon, for instance, has over 17.5 miles of hallways, it only takes about seven minutes to walk between any two points within the facility! Originally built on unwanted property—the area consisted of landfills and wastelands that no one wished to develop—the Pentagon has evolved into a unique government entity. It has all of the resources and services needed to be self-contained. Consider the following facts about the Pentagon:

- 23,000 employees daily consume 4,500 cups of coffee; 1,700 pints of milk; 6,800 soft drinks; and make 200,000 phone calls over 100,000 miles of phone cable. About 1.2 million pieces of mail are processed every month!

- The total land area of the Pentagon is 583 acres with 16 parking lots for over 8,700 vehicles.

- Inside the Pentagon, there are 121 stairways, 19 escalators, 13 elevators, 284 restrooms, 691 drinking fountains, over 7,700 windows, and 4,200 clocks!

No one back in 1941 could have foreseen that the start of this structure would result in the creation of a government landmark. All seventeen buildings of the early War Department are found within the Pentagon. It supports and meets the daily work and personal needs of its large civilian and military staffs. Within its confines, decisions are made about our national state of readiness, the placement of armed forces, and the conduct of wars, starting with World War II up to the present day. The Pentagon truly is a city unto itself with a single mission—to provide for the common defense of the nation.

Name: _____ Date: _____

Bits and Pieces of Politics

Directions: Try your luck in figuring out these odd "bits and pieces" of political trivia. If you can answer half of the questions below correctly, you can consider yourself a trivia authority!

1. **Question:** What famous national symbol was hidden in the floorboards of the Zion Reformed Church in Allentown, Pennsylvania, to avoid being melted down and made into a cannon by the British?

   Answer: _____

2. **Question:** What two presidents also had sons who became U.S. presidents?

   Answer: _____

3. **Question:** Why didn't Maryland secede from the Union in 1865?

   Answer: _____

4. **Question:** What president spoke Chinese with his wife when they did not wish to be overheard while in the White House?

   Answer: _____

5. **Question:** Who was the first African-American woman elected to the Senate?

   Answer: _____

6. **Question:** What colony (state) was the first to legalize witchcraft?

   Answer: _____

7. **Question:** Who does "I like Ike" refer to?

   Answer: _____

8. **Question:** What presidential hopeful was severely wounded in an assassination attempt in 1972 but still won two Democratic primaries the next day (Michigan and Maryland)?

   Answer: _____

9. **Question:** Which president set three unique records while in office?

   Answer: _____

10. **Question:** What were the three records?

    Answer: A. _____

    B. _____

    C. _____

11. **Question:** What is Antonia Nathan famous for?

    Answer: _____

Federal Bureaucracy

Think of the federal government as a business whose purpose is to manage the affairs of a nation. These affairs or interests include the legislative, executive, judicial, and administrative branches of government. This fourth branch, the **administrative branch**, consists of all the agencies, groups, and organizations that "run the country." Rules and regulations, executive orders, laws, and court decisions make it possible for the administrative branch to conduct business. This branch has been assigned various powers to "make things happen." The Postal Service, for instance, is responsible for matters relating to the mail (e.g., issuing postage stamps, delivery, and storage). The Border Patrol, as a second example, is charged with enforcing federal laws regulating our national borders, among them the capture of illegal aliens and the theft of technology.

Money fuels all of these endeavors. The government as a corporation spends and receives enormous amounts of revenue (See Money, Money, Money …). The revenue is used for production and service. **Production** refers to things created by the federal government to help achieve a goal, e.g., aircraft carriers, setting aside property as wilderness, and maintaining a reserve fuel supply. **Service** means the use or application of federal products or resources, e.g., tax audits, operating federal prisons, and managing the Social Security program. All of these activities are operated by a **bureaucracy** (an organization with a chain of command, a pyramidal form, and governed by rules and procedures). That is to say, information and decisions tend to move down the chain of command. The typical bureaucracy has one chief, several assistants, and staff. There are several million people employed by the federal government who provide some type of product or service for citizens.

These employees work under the rules of the **Civil Service System**. They are hired through competitive exams and abide by a standard set of regulations regarding federal employees. Pay raises and promotions, for instance, are based on designated scales and steps. Civil Service, therefore, is meant to reduce the risk of patronage and corruption in government by using rules that apply to all employees, e.g., code of conduct. The result is that these persons basically enact the policies and programs of each department and each has a part to play. AMTRAK, the Tennessee Valley Authority, the National Aeronautics and Space Administration (NASA), and the General Services Administration (GSA) are practical examples of government "**corporations**" operated by federal employees that fulfill a need for production or service. These are just a few in a long list of departments, agencies, and corporations that manage the many business concerns of the federal government. It is the federal employee, moreover, who handles the daily routine of our national "business."

Money, Money, Money ...

It is very common for families and individuals to create a budget. A budget is a break-down of how much money is earned versus how much money is needed to pay bills and other costs or expenditures. The federal government must have its own budget. The president and Congress, in a sense, set up an annual budget for the nation. It is based upon how much revenue the government anticipates making from taxpayers and other sources. This estimate is compared to the amount necessary to "run the government" and achieve its goals. These goals include a wide array of activities such as law enforcement, scientific research, foreign aid, and health care.

Did You Know That ...

 Personal income taxes accounted for $1 trillion in 2000? Corporate taxes totaled $207 billion. About half of the government's revenue flow is derived from individual income taxes!

Like a family, the federal government must pay its bills. To do so, it depends primarily on taxes. When revenues exceed spending, we call it a **surplus**. When spending is greater than available revenues, it is known as a **deficit**. The government acquires its revenues from these basic sources:

- Corporate income taxes,
- Individual income taxes,
- Social insurance payroll taxes (e.g., unemployment insurance, Social Security),
- Excise taxes on luxuries (e.g., alcohol and other products), and
- Other taxes (miscellaneous), such as customs duties and estate taxes.

It is estimated that the government will receive about $2.2 trillion in revenues for 2001–2002. If so, a portion of the projected surplus for that period may be used to reduce the **national debt** or deficit. The national debt is, in essence, a very large amount of money that the federal government owes to its lenders (yes, the government borrows money in much the same way as families).

The biggest items in the government's budget are Social Security (23%), national defense (16%), discretionary projects (19%), and Medicare (12%). This means that approximately 70% of all the revenue that enters the national budget is slated to be spent for four expenditures. The eventual goal of the budgeting process is to make a **balanced budget** in which income (taxes) equals costs (expenditures) on an annual basis with a reservoir of extra money (savings) set aside for future needs or emergencies. Think of it like this—all the bills in the family get paid, and a savings account is created.

The U.S. Census

Article 1, Section 2 of the U.S. Constitution requires that we conduct a national **census** (head count) of the population every ten years in order to tally how many people reside within the United States. That figure should include men, women, and children of all ages. The most recent was Census 2000, which tallied over 281 million people living in America.

Although the census was initially done on horseback, modern census-taking has replaced mounted officials with computers, mailed questionnaires, and the use of data processing. The survey results are collected and carefully sifted through by experts. They compile the results in published, easy-to-understand forms and reports that explain a number of characteristics about our nation's population. Our national census is a valuable tool. The census numbers:

- Decide how many seats each state will have in its state legislature and in the U.S. House of Representatives.

- Determine the levels of federal and state funds for all types of important community projects, such as new schools, highways, and industrial parks.

- Are used by businesses and industries to decide where to locate their factories, shopping malls, and other services. Those decisions can have a major impact on employment.

- Are relied upon by cities and counties to decide where to allocate their limited resources for maximum benefit. Increased population growth, for instance, in one area may produce overcrowded schools. This, in turn, may compel local authorities to subdivide, which could mean a student is bussed a greater distance to a different, less-crowded school.

No matter what its uses, the national census is a critical element in shaping the growth of the nation. Virtually every agency and department of local, state, and federal government rely on the census figures to make decisions as far-reaching as where to open a military base in Alaska or begin drilling for oil in Utah. The data included in the census is economic, social, political, and geographic—all districts, all states, and over eight million city blocks are included in the final tally. You name it, and it's probably available somewhere in the census's documents and numbers!

Did You Know That ...

 The first census was done on horseback by 17 U.S. Marshals and approximately 200 aides? They used quill pens, bottled ink, and bits of paper to record their numbers. They traveled around the newly-formed states counting heads, about four million of them. The whole endeavor is estimated to have cost about $45,000.

Name: _____ Date: _____

Running the Country: Word Search

Directions: Find and circle the words listed below in the word search puzzle. Words may be printed forward, backward, up, down, or diagonally.

```
M P G R L S T N E M T R A P E D U N D U I V J X
E E B N R M D A H C J A E W U J O R O B K W B F
T I X X I E M K L M I D Y R K Y I F L K W B H V
S D D Q J N B M X T X V H T A S E I C N E G A Y
Y E F B E R O V X V Y D R H F X U Z Q I S X M T
S X I X G H S F K L K Y P E S R Z Z B B T V L Y
T L E I X P A D E F I C I T S B S T D Y A Z G C
I S U L P R U S B Y V R P U N L Y P B J P F Q A
R Q E H H B M X P P Q X P N Q V I O E W K P T R
E I Z R E G U L A T I O N S X F Y V U A P L X C
M Z Y B E N Z C F X S B Z Q A B C P I Z S W Y U
S G N U S P E F R X Z Q I S Q T E S M C U N F A
X N O I T A R T S I N I M D A D C I Y R K U L E
R N B Z H G X O K Z G U O K B R O S W S V B M R
I G Y C U G F A S E S U A L C E C R E M M O C U
R S B H J S U Q W C T S G K Q M K G F F V R R B
I N G R O S S N A T I O N A L P R O D U C T U A
G X S M V A I E X O X Y S P B R J Z P Y W X P M
U B U D G E T K X H U M L Z E D I N J K Y X Z S
S M H S W G I O L L E J Z N L K F R R P M V H E
L F E C H A T I E V R E S E R L A R E D E F H X
C L W S Y E Z Q W B A B I F O C X N V T G N M A
A L F U L L F A I T H A N D C R E D I T Y Y I T
P M A R J V X U C U N H U A G Q N N R B Z U F W
```

WORD LIST

Administration	Agencies	Budget
Bureaucracy	Civil Service	Commerce Clause
Deficit	Departments	Federal Reserve
Full Faith and Credit	Gross National Product	Merit System
Regulations	Surplus	Taxes

Public Opinion

Public opinion is the collective viewpoint of a large number of people about an issue. Opinions cannot be scientifically verified. They reflect personal or private attitudes toward a topic. To better understand public opinion, we should consider the following factors:

- **Strength of conviction or intensity:** How strongly do groups of people feel about an issue? Does a group, for instance, launch a public relations campaign against teenage smoking?

- **Longevity:** Are the opinions fairly stable within the group, or do they shift over time?

- **Size of group:** How many citizens agree/disagree on an issue of common concern? Small groups are rarely heard unless it is a volatile issue like school safety. The larger the **constituency** (group) who share a consensus of attitudes, the more likely the group will be heard by decision-makers.

- **Issue effect:** How many people are affected and to what degree by the issue(s)?

Because public opinion is essential to our system of government—it tells us what most people like, dislike, or feel neutral about—we need a way to measure it. Attitude and opinion research is widely used by business and government agencies to gauge public opinion on an endless array of topics as diverse as sporting goods, television shows, taxations, and legalizing marijuana. Polls and surveys are used to test public opinion. We participate in these polls through interviews, questionnaires, and different types of samples.

An organized group that tries to influence government decisions and policies is called an **interest group** or **lobby**. Interest groups try to measure and influence public opinion for their cause. Interest groups, furthermore, seek to manipulate the **mass media** (e.g., television, radio, Internet), to shape public attitudes. The National Rifle Association (NRA), for example, strives to protect the rights of gun owners. It does so by lobbying, using the media, conducting surveys, and proposing legislation.

As the saying goes, "Everyone has an opinion on something." In a democratic system of government, public opinion is critical. It affirms the belief that the government's right to rule is drawn from the consent of the people. Public opinion is simply the means by which the citizenry or **electorate** (voters) voice their attitudes and values (loudly enough to be heard) on issues that matter.

Name: _____ Date: _____

Case Study: Should English Be Adopted as the National Language?

The United States is a nation of over 281 million citizens with virtually every language represented in homes, at work, in school, and in places of worship. It is a composite nation of all types of people from all points of the globe, from Albania to Zimbabwe. In fact, millions of legal immigrants have arrived in America during the past several decades, bringing with them their values, beliefs, customs, and above all else—their languages.

In this exercise you are asked to make a difficult decision. Should we adopt English as our national language? In other words, should proficiency in English be a requirement for all people who wish to live and work and be educated as citizens in this country? An effective way to organize your decision is to list the pros and cons, the strengths and weaknesses of the issue. Below is a short list for you to insert your views in the appropriate categories. Compare those points of view with your classmates before making a final decision on this tricky issue.

PROS

1. _____
2. _____
3. _____
4. _____
5. _____

CONS

1. _____
2. _____
3. _____
4. _____
5. _____

DECISION

_____

_____

_____

_____

_____

Name: _____ Date: _____

Sense and Nonsense

Read carefully through the scenario below. It has 12 mistakes (at least) relating to government in the United States. Briefly jot down the errors and the correct answer(s) on the lines provided. Good luck.

The ten U.S. Supreme Court judges sat at the conference table discussing many issues. "Democracy means that only certain people are above the law. We are those people," Justice Bones argued.

"Are you kidding?" replied Justice Myers. "The Bill of Rights clearly states that the government is supreme in all things. No one, no state, no group may ever override the federal government."

"Wrong. Federalism allows us to separate powers so that a state is as powerful as the federal government. After all, that's why Congress and the states have concurrent powers," Justice Bones retorted. He was angry at any type of opposition to his viewpoints. "If people want things changed, they can hold an election at any time and vote in change. You know, I kind of admire third parties—they are usually successful in getting candidates elected who change things and promote justice, especially in the presidential elections."

"Colleagues," interrupted Chief Justice Scott, "speaking of the president, we must attend to our duties to enforce the laws of the land. The president announced yesterday that he intended to sponsor a filibuster in the Cabinet. It is our duty to make sure that the Cabinet does not try to impose a caucus on Congress. Where would we be if the president were allowed to gerrymander the public to vote for his proposals? I suggest that we draft a writ of certiorari to announce our opposition to the president's plans. I expect no obstacles. Besides, we have jurisdiction over all types of cases!"

ERRORS

1. _____
2. _____
3. _____
4. _____
5. _____
6. _____
7. _____
8. _____
9. _____
10. _____
11. _____
12. _____

State Government

All 50 states differ in matters such as climate, population, size, culture, history, and economic base. They are alike, however, in one very important respect—their system of government. Every state has a structure of government that includes a constitution with a preamble and bill of rights, three branches of government, a state bureaucracy with departments and agencies, and the use of elections.

As was mentioned in the section on federalism, there is a division of powers in this country. Any issues that affect the nation and its people are generally left to the authority or jurisdiction of the federal government. These include, among others, the powers to conduct foreign affairs, to make money, and to provide for our national defense. States, on the other hand, attend to issues that happen exclusively within their respective borders. The state of Illinois, for example, cannot interfere in government decisions in other states. Normally, a state has authority or powers in areas such as education (public schools), highways, criminal justice, health/safety, and public works. Money for these various projects and programs is derived from state taxes (e.g., income, corporate, sales, and property). This leads us to the notion of **shared or concurrent powers**. States share certain powers with the federal government. Taxation is perhaps the most important and necessary of these shared powers. Without the power to tax its citizens, a state could not fulfill its duties. In addition, states enter into agreement with the **Full Faith and Credit Clause** in Article 4, Section 1, of the Constitution. This clause requires that states honor the decisions of each other's courts. A marriage certificate issued in New Mexico will be accepted in New Jersey. A tourist using a credit card in Alaska may do so, even though he or she resides in Alabama. This clause, an agreement between states, enables commerce to occur, contracts to be signed and upheld, and daily life to transpire within and among states.

The organization of each state government is relatively simple. The executive branch consists of a **governor** and **lieutenant governor** and a host of state executive agencies (e.g., **secretary of state**). He or she is assisted by a Cabinet and a cadre or core of political party advisors. The powers of a governor as chief executive are varied; these duties include:

- Drafting a budget for the state,
- Appointing officials to state agencies (with the consent of the state Senate),
- Proposing legislation,
- Serving as the symbolic chief of state,
- Approving or vetoing bills put forth by the state legislature,
- Attending ceremonial functions,
- Administering the activities of the executive agencies, and
- Supervising the state police.

State Government (cont.)

All state legislatures, except Nebraska, have a **bicameral** (two-house) legislature. This approach is meant to allow the state House of Representatives and state Senate to serve as checks on each other. The basic function of the legislators is, of course, to enact legislation on matters that pertain to the health, welfare, and safety of the state. This is done through a law-making process comparable to that used in the U.S. Congress. Committees review proposals and make recommendations. A bill is sent back and forth between the two Houses until either a consensus is reached or the proposal is "quashed." In some states, citizens have a chance to participate directly in the lawmaking process through the use of a **referendum** or an **initiative**. A referendum means that a **statute** (law) or possibly a proposed law is sent to the voters for approval or rejection. The initiative enables voters to circumvent or bypass a legislature that does not act on something of great importance, such as legalized gambling. A **petition** signed by about 10 to 15 percent of the people who voted in the previous general election is needed to put an issue on the ballot. The initiative either succeeds or fails, depending on the voter turnout and support (or lack of). Thus we find that, throughout the nation, every state has a legislative body, and many have "alternative" methods for giving voters the opportunity to pass legislation.

The final branch of state government is the **judiciary**. Unlike the legislative and executive branches, the judicial systems of the fifty states are all different. Their basic functions, however, are identical: to interpret and apply state laws.

A typical state court system has four layers:

1. **Lower Courts:** hear traffic, juvenile, family, magistrate, and small claims cases.
2. **General Trial Courts:** hear felony and major civil cases.
3. **Appeals Courts:** Hear appeals from the general trial and lower courts.
4. **State Supreme Court** (also known as the Court of Last Resort): Is the highest court of appeals in a state.

These courts preside over **criminal and civil cases** based on their jurisdiction or authority to hear certain types of issues. A juvenile court judge, for example, would not be authorized to review a case of manslaughter by an adult. Criminal courts deal exclusively with violations of law in the form of **misdemeanors** (minor crimes) and **felonies** (major offenses). A guilty person may be punished with **incarceration** (jail/prison), fines, community service, probation, or, even in some cases, death. Civil courts handle cases involving disagreements between persons, groups, and/or organizations, including governments and businesses. The "loser" in civil court must pay a financial penalty to the other party or person in the case. The ultimate goal in all instances, civil or criminal, is to ensure that justice and fairness are served within the state court system.

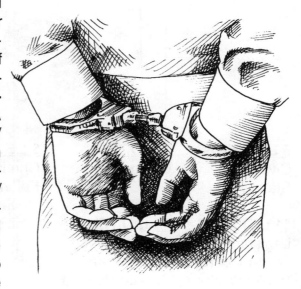

Name: _____ Date: _____

State Government: Kriss Kross

Directions: Use a pencil for this puzzle. Fit the words from the list below in the correct spaces below. There may be two words that fit in the same boxes, but if you are unable to connect the next word, you know you have written in the wrong word. If so, then erase and continue with the other word that does fit.

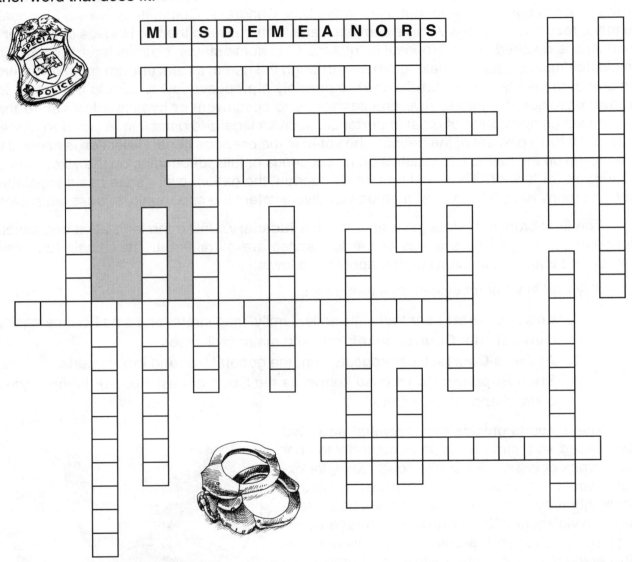

M I S D E M E A N O R S

5 LETTERS	**7 LETTERS**	**8 LETTERS**	**9 LETTERS**	**10 LETTERS**
Civil	Cabinet	Criminal	Bicameral	Initiative
State		Felonies	Education	Referendum
		Governor		
		Petition		

11 LETTERS	**12 LETTERS**		**16 LETTERS**	
Legislature	Appeals Court		Secretary of State	
Lower Courts	Misdemeanors			
Public Works	Shared Powers		**18 LETTERS**	
	Supreme Court		Full Faith and Credit	

What a Difference a State Makes!

Each state wields a certain amount of political clout based on its size. Remember that states with higher populations have more representatives in Congress; thus, they have more votes to cast on issues and legislation. Each state also has its own government, structure, and organization based on its history, location, culture, and people. Let's take a look at some of the fundamental differences between four state governments.

	LOUISIANA	MISSOURI	CALIFORNIA	MAINE
Capital	Baton Rouge	Jefferson City	Sacramento	Augusta
Area (sq. mi.)	43,567	68,898	1,555,974	30,865
Population	4,468,976	5,595,211	33,871,648	1,274,923
Admission	1812	1821	1850	1820
Governor				
Term	4 years	4 years	4 years	4 years
Term Limit	2 terms	2 terms	2 terms	2 terms
Salary	$95,000	$94,564	$120,000	$70,000
HOUSE				
No. Reps.	106	163	80	153
Term	4 years	2 years	2 years	2 years
Term Limit	3 terms	4 terms	3 terms	4 terms
SENATE				
No. Senators	39	34	40	35
Term	4 years	4 years	4 years	4 years
Term Limit	3 terms	2 terms	2 terms	4 terms
SUPREME CT.				
No. Justices	7	7	7	7
Term	10 years	12 years	12 years	7 years
Local Govt.	64 parishes (counties)	114 counties	58 counties	16 counties

Name: _____ Date: _____

Case Study: Should a Confederate Flag Be Flown at a State Capitol?

The flag of the Confederate States of America (C.S.A.) has hung outside many government buildings in southern states at different times during the past five decades. Curiously enough, this flag is not a national flag but one used in battle. It was created by General P.G.T. Beauregard for use in battle by Southern troops in the Civil War. Since then, its usage has evoked strong feelings and reactions. To African-Americans, the C.S.A. flag is a glaring symbol and reminder of bigotry, slavery, and a legacy of oppression. To advocates, the flag is a proud symbol of states' rights and independence. In the summer of 2000, the state of South Carolina—once a slave state—was confronted with the volatile issue of a Confederate flag flown from the capitol dome. After fierce debate and demonstrations by both sides, the state legislature moved the flag to a war monument on state property.

This incident shows how a symbol can provoke public opinion and spark racial intolerance, especially one that dates back over 100 years. A flag, by the way, is a type of symbolic speech—no words are spoken, but the image ignites debate. For instance, imagine if someone wanted to hang a Nazi flag atop a public building in a predominantly Jewish community! In a sense, therefore, the Civil War may be over, but its legacy lives on in the Confederate flag.

So, here is the challenge in the form of a two-part exercise.

Issues

1. Decide when, if ever, a Confederate flag should be allowed to hang on state property. Explain why.

_____

_____

_____

_____

_____

_____

2. Did the state of South Carolina make the right decision? Why or why not?

_____

_____

_____

_____

_____

Local Government

The simplest way to discuss local government is to view it as a miniature version of state government. States are organized geographically and politically by administrative units called **counties** and **municipalities**. A **county** is a geographic region with a county government (usually located in a county courthouse). There are over 3,000 counties in America. Within each county there are specific municipal sites referred to as cities, towns, villages, and districts (school and special). These combine for about 80,000 sites. States provide the laws and **charters** that give local governments the power to operate.

A county is a major political arm of state government. Many counties are very large and heavily populated, e.g., Cook County in Illinois and San Diego County in California. These counties require a very complex administrative agency.

Some of the many functions of a county are to:

• Administer state social services (e.g., foster care, food stamps, vaccinations, etc.).

• Uphold state laws and operate regional criminal justice facilities, such as courts and jails.

• Record all state-mandated documents within the county (e.g., marriage/birth certificates, housing/land permits, and court information).

• Maintain public facilities including roads, libraries, bridges, and hospitals.

• Administer elections and voter registration.

To fulfill these duties, a county is managed by a governing board often known as a **board of commissioners**. A board is an executive group with limited powers to pass rules and regulations. Other officials exist to help conduct the business of the county. Most of these public officials in the following sample should seem familiar.

• **Sheriff:** serves as the chief law-enforcement officer of the county.

• **Treasurer/Collector:** oversees the county taxes and revenues.

• **Prosecuting/District Attorney:** serves as the agent of the state government in county trials.

• **Coroner/Medical Examiner:** serves as a "death detective" and supervises the county morgue.

• **Clerk of Courts:** paperwork/record keeper of area courts.

Local Government (cont.)

Municipalities or cities/towns, on the other hand, appear in a thousand different styles, sizes, and appearances. Some are so small as to barely constitute a medieval village of 200 residents. Others, like New York City, San Francisco, and Phoenix are so vast as to engulf every village-sized municipality in the country. By modern standards, a **city** is seen as the largest example of a municipality. It is a unit of government that includes virtually every type of service needed to operate a congested, thriving population. A city provides for the routine, daily needs and services of its inhabitants. These services include, among others, water/sewage treatment plants, police, hospitals, schools, highways, utilities, trash collection, parks, museums, and the development of tourist sites. A major metropolitan area like a city is self-contained; everything a citizen needs to live his or her life is found within the city limits, from employment to fine dining to recreation.

Although municipalities are unique, we can recognize four basic forms or styles of government:

- **Council-Manager:** An elected council oversees the actions of a city manager who, in turn, is the operational chief.

- **Mayor-Council "strong":** The mayor is the city executive, and the council serves as the local legislature (e.g., it passes ordinances and supervises finances).

- **Commission:** A small group of elected officials administers all functions of the city government through consensus.

- **Mayor-Council "symbolic or weak":** The mayor presides over a city council that serves as the executive/legislative decision-makers.
This style often incorporates a city manager to carry out day-to-day duties.

All four styles are known as "**grassroots politics.**" They represent the lowest level at which citizens can get involved in government affairs. There are no further levels or intermediate groups to block a voter's access to his or her elected officials. Additionally, it is at the local level of government that we are typically affected, e.g., garbage collection, disaster relief, ambulance service, and school lunch programs. It is a critical duty of all city governments, therefore, to see that the fundamental safety, welfare, and general peace of their jurisdictions are preserved.

Local Government: Word Scrambler

Directions: Unscramble the words below using the words in the word bank.

charter	city manager	collector	commissioner
coroner	council	county	district
jails	mayor	municipalities	prosecutor
sheriff	village	voter registration	

1. YOAMR _____

2. TTRDCISI _____

3. SMNIEIUICLAPIT _____

4. TCNYUO _____

5. ELLIGAV _____

6. TROVE NGOEIRSRTITA _____

7. SLAJI _____

8. TARHRCE _____

9. ROORPUSETC _____

10. SCMIIOOMNRES _____

11. RFSFEIH _____

12. NOORREC _____

13. YICT RGAAMEN _____

14. CLONUCI _____

15. ROOCELLCT _____

67

Name: _____ Date: _____

Some Days It Pays to Stay in Bed!

There are two types of mayors—"strong" and "weak or symbolic." A strong mayor has lawful powers to act as a chief executive for his or her municipality, whereas a "weak" mayor simply presides over a city council whose members serve as the decision-makers.

Imagine that you are the mayor of Smileyville, a small rural town of 3,000. In the course of **ONE WEEK**, the following events are brought to your attention. Consider each of these "incidents" and decide what to do. Keep two things in mind as you proceed: (1) no matter what you do, someone or some group will be displeased, and (2) **all of these events are true!**

Incident 1: A small Amish community lives on the outskirts of town. The members enter your town often to buy supplies, medicines, and so on. They are always willing to help with town projects (at no cost). Their leader has asked for hitching posts for their carriages to be placed at town expense at several points. Some citizens dislike the Amish because their horses "pollute the city," and the Amish do not pay local property taxes. What do you do?

_____

_____

_____

_____

Incident 2: Your city clerk enters toting a 25-pound howitzer shell that a farmer found protruding from a ditch. The shell is live and capable of exploding. She places it on your desk and exits (in a hurry!). What do you do?

_____

_____

_____

_____

Incident 3: A high school boy teased a loose dog. The dog bit the boy. State law requires that the dog be captured and tested for rabies. The dog is running loose somewhere in town and has avoided all of the traps. To catch it means that it must be shot, probably within the city limits. The townspeople are fearful of the dog and of being shot by accident by the police. What do you do?

_____

_____

_____

_____

Name: _____ Date: _____

Some Days It Pays to Stay in Bed! (cont.)

Incident 4: The local (and only) newspaper refuses to print your "Mayor's Column" for free. You use your column to inform citizens of decisions and activities of your office and city government. The newspaper, however, does publish at no cost the newsletters sent to it from the state senator and representative from your district. You are all publicly-elected officials. Why should the mayor pay, with city funds, to have a column printed? What do you do?

_____

_____

_____

_____

Incident 5: Junk and abandoned cars are a health and safety risk to your town, e.g., they attract rats. Also, they look terrible! You issue an announcement that all junk cars must be removed from public streets. A local militia member threatens to shoot to kill anyone who tries to remove his two junk vehicles that are located on a city street. What do you do?

_____

_____

_____

_____

Incident 6: You arrange to purchase, with grant money, a drug dog to help the police combat drug abuse in Smileyville. The dog is instrumental in identifying several makers and users of various drugs. Some citizens protest that the dog is an invasion of privacy and that the mayor had no right to purchase one. What do you do?

_____

_____

_____

_____

Incident 7: There is a small liberal arts college on a hilltop overlooking the town. A group of college students asks for a permit to host a volleyball tournament in a city park. The tournament is a fundraiser to help raise money for college scholarships. Residents argue that the students will drink beer and play loud music while playing volleyball and demand that the permit not be issued. What do you do?

_____

_____

_____

_____

Name: _____ Date: _____

Feeling Lucky?: Policy Into Practice

Times seem to be getting tougher and tougher in Smileyville, USA. The chief of police has notified you (the mayor) that a new gang called "Double Trouble" is forming. The gang has about 25 members and consists of males ages 14 to 19 who have dropped out of school. They specialize in car theft, "hit and run" robberies at local stores, and terrorizing area high school students. The press is howling for action. Citizens' groups are complaining (loudly) about how ineffective city government is in dealing with this problem.

Something must be done! The first step is to draft and implement a policy. A **policy** is a plan designed to produce a course of action. In this case, the challenge is clear—what type of policy is needed to put an end to "Double Trouble"? To do nothing or very little will only aggravate the situation. Gangs are a blight in every major city. They destroy local communities and produce nothing of lasting value.

You are the mayor of the city of Smileyville. Use the following statement, written in the form of a public address, to create a policy that will address the escalating gang problem.

Gang Policy

"Ladies and gentlemen, citizens of Smileyville, I have carefully considered the growing problem of gangs in our city. It is my decision to implement a policy that will neutralize the gangs. I firmly believe that we can do so by

_____

_____

_____

_____

_____

_____

_____

This policy is, in my opinion, likely to prove extremely effective because it _____

_____

_____

_____

_____

_____

Name: _____   Date: _____

Principles of Government: Master Blaster Crossword

Directions: Use the clues below to complete the crossword puzzle.

ACROSS

3. A Latin phrase meaning where you are born decides your citizenship (two words)
6. Immigrants use this formal process to become citizens
9. Think "separation of powers"
14. Citizens own the government (two words)
15. Majority rule with concern for minority issues and views
16. Group who drafted a government-making document (two words)

DOWN

1. General agreement on an issue
2. One way to amend the Constitution (three words)
4. "Give me your tired, your poor ..." (three words)
5. "To form a more perfect union ..."
7. Elected officials pay attention to this group
8. Powers left to the states by the federal government
10. Additions to the Constitution
11. First ten amendments to the Constitution
12. Basic principle of democracy
13. Powers shared by the federal and state governments

    71

Name: _____ Date: _____

★ Branches of Government: Master Blaster Crossword

Directions: Use the clues below to complete the crossword puzzle.

ACROSS

8. A Latin term meaning a law passed "after the fact" (three words)
10. Groups that handle legislation in Congress
12. Proposed law
14. Redrawing district lines to get the vote
16. Serves 6 years, not 2

DOWN

1. Legislator running for reelection
2. To reject or refuse to sign a bill
3. Presides over the House of Representatives
4. Period of work in Congress
5. Put both Houses together, and what do you get?
6. Power to remove a government official
7. Congress can't pass one to "getcha" (three words)
9. "Enough talk. Let's vote!" (three words)
11. When you just can't get a legislator to shut up and sit down
13. A body of Congress
15. Congressional schedule of bills

Name: _____ Date: _____

Campaigns, Parties, Elections: Master Blaster Crossword

Directions: Use the clues below to complete the crossword puzzle.

ACROSS
1. Presidential voting delegates (two words)
5. All of the same party on one ticket
9. Sign up to vote
10. We copied the Australian version of this
11. Not the sort you walk on but part of a platform
13. Not a Democrat
16. Official assembly for a political party

DOWN
2. Temporary unions of diverse political interests
3. A means of voting for someone
4. Ralph Nader was a candidate for one of these (two words)
6. Length of office
7. A place where you go to vote (two words)
8. A person running for office
12. Party list of candidates running for office
14. Local voting district found in cities
15. Contest to win an election

Name: _____   Date: _____

 American Government: Grand Master Word Search

Directions: Find and circle the words listed below in the word search puzzle. Words may be printed forward, backward, up, down, or diagonally.

```
O A P R Y Z C Y I P Z V L G E O J N E V P Z G Z
C G U U Y G O A M E R I C A N F L A G A T O C L
B P L L I Y N T R K O I I Y G X X D Y J V K O U
E O F E N R S R T R U O C E M E R P U S W E D C
Q W N O P N T G D I G I Y U M L U V P H Q K K P
R E K F P E I N B U R E A U C R A C Y W M D D F
C R A F Y M T I U D R P G E L E C T O R A T E R
X S H O S Y U R R C L A N F S O B O G S N W N V
L L C U L U T A C R V G I R K Q H I Q O O R O R
F I M R P G I G S R F C A H R J W X L C X I I G
O L S E L W O T L L K M U P H Y B S K L S A T M
U T J H C U N P F B E A B C R O N R E V O G A G
N X F D D B A L U N E A I B C S D C V Z Q B T F
D R Q V N N L L D B W Q T D G Q E J S A I P N X
I U C J E X E M Z V L B W S U S N E C L E A E M
N E C O Q T E T V X A I T T S G D F L W O G S X
G T C M E N O S B I R I C R B G P O W L J I E S
F A Y X T Y M O S I M W S O J V F H P B L H R M
A B E S D Q H Q G J V L V G P R Y H U A V P P D
T E O H W H I T E H O U S E I I E P R T U W E H
H D W I Z P O T B P B P C G Q B N E L F N E R X
E U A A V B L R O X E Y H G M R D I H U P S P R
R H J C O N G R E S S T P Q M E N L O N Y Q R Z
S E Q O B C B S S R S J C X F L M E V N K Q T A
```

WORD LIST

Amendments	American Flag	Bill
Bill of Rights	Bureaucracy	Census
Congress	Constitutional	Debate
Electorate	Federalism	Founding Fathers
Governor	Powers	Public Opinion
Representation	Rule of Four	Supreme Court
Veto	White House	

74

Name: _____ Date: _____

American Government: Grand Master Kriss Kross

Directions: Use a pencil for this puzzle. Fit the words from the list below in the correct spaces below. There may be two words that fit in the same boxes, but if you are unable to connect the next word, you know you have written in the wrong word. If so, then erase and continue with the other word that does fit.

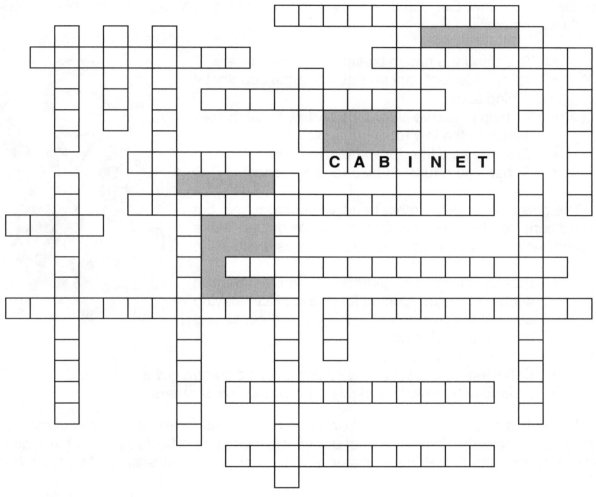

3 LETTERS	**4 LETTERS**	**5 LETTERS**	**6 LETTERS**	**7 LETTERS**
Law	Bill	House	Census	Cabinet
	Veto	Mayor	Senate	

8 LETTERS	**9 LETTERS**	**10 LETTERS**	**11 LETTERS**	**12 LETTERS**
Equality	Candidate	Convention	Bureaucracy	American Flag
	Democracy	Electorate	Citizenship	Bill of Rights
	President	Oval Office	Liberty Bell	Jurisdiction
				Supreme Court

14 LETTERS	**15 LETTERS**
Judicial Review	Founding Fathers
	Statue of Liberty

75

A Citizen's Primer

Citizenship is not free. An American citizen has certain **duties and obligations** to fulfill. The Constitution, federal and state laws, court decisions, city ordinances, and the rules and regulations of the nation combine to guarantee each citizen many freedoms. These freedoms include such rights as the right to life, free speech, religion, vote, and protection from unfair prosecution by the law. Our duties, however, are the mandatory expectations of each citizen. These duties include:

- To defend the nation by service in the military.
- To provide for financial stability of the country by paying taxes.
- To help preserve an orderly society through obedience to the law (criminal and civil).
- To serve as a juror or witness in court.
- To become educated by attending school.

The obligations, on the other hand, are not required, but we should consider them as equally important as duties. These obligations begin the day we achieve legal status as an adult by:

- Paying attention to politics and government in such matters as running for public office, staying abreast of government activities, and contacting one's representatives.
- Voting! Voting! Voting!
- Behaving as a responsible citizen of one's community and state.
- Defending the welfare, rights, and well-being of others.

The duties and obligations are few, but they are vital to the long-term success of our government and society. The success of our efforts thus far is reflected in the observations of Jawaharlal Nehru, the first Prime Minister of India, about the character of American citizens (1949):

"The picture of the average American presented to the outside world is of a hardheaded, efficient, and practical businessman, intent on making money and using that money to add to his power and influence. That picture, no doubt, has some truth in it. And yet there is another picture, and I think, a much more enduring one, of a warmhearted and very generous people, full of good will to others and with a firm belief in the basic principles on which this great republic was founded— the principles of freedom, equality, and democracy ... Everywhere I have found a love of freedom and a desire for peace and cooperation and among the people, a frankness and human approach which make a friendly understanding easier.

During these wanderings of mine, I have noticed the great variety of American life and, at the same time, the fundamental unity of it."

September 11, 2001

"One country, one Constitution, one destiny."   —Daniel Webster

On September 11, 2001, foreign terrorists launched a several-pronged assault on the United States. Four commercial airliners were hijacked and used as aerial firebombs to destroy the twin towers of the World Trade Center in New York City and a section of the Pentagon in Washington, D.C. The fourth plane crashed in a Pennsylvania field, after heroic efforts by crew and passengers to retake control. Several thousand people died within the space of a few hours as the world watched, shocked at the enormity of these attacks on American soil. It represented the first full-scale enemy offensive conducted within the borders of the continental United States since the War of 1812. This enemy offensive was led by Osama bin Laden and others, supported by the Taliban dictatorship of Afghanistan, and executed by al-Qaeda terrorists, including foreign Islamic mercenaries from the Middle East and Africa. Their goals were to annihilate the government of the United States, to destroy the capitalist system of free enterprise, and to bring the 281 million citizens of this country to ruin.

These antagonists or opponents are opposed to virtually everything the United States represents—freedom, equality, representation, and opportunity. Their militant version of Islamic "liberation" meant, quite simply, that those who did not submit to the word of Allah must die in a **jihad** (holy war). After the attacks, the national economy began a steady decline. The country's armed forces were put on full alert in anticipation of additional attacks. On the heels of these atrocities, lethal amounts of anthrax were being sent to branches of the government and the mass media by person(s) or parties unknown. Congress and the Supreme Court were forced to relocate their workplaces in order to avoid the distinct risk of anthrax contamination. Citizens died or were made ill from exposure to the disease.

Within several weeks of the attacks, President George W. Bush announced that the United States would attack terrorism wherever it was uncovered. Afghanistan became the focus of our endeavors. A military alliance was formed with opposition forces in Afghanistan. Partnerships were cemented with Pakistan, China, Russia, England, and other world powers to isolate Afghanistan's dictatorship. The subsequent offensive resulted in the overthrow of the Taliban regime and the takeover of the country. Civilians, soldiers, and terrorists died in the process. America learned a bitter, lasting lesson—that some of the world's nations and cultures despise democracy and everything our Constitution represents. These cultures resent our prosperity and want to "level the playing field" by leveling the United States.

September 11, 2001, however, did succeed in uniting our nation. Our legacy is one of achievement and one of violence. September 11, 2001, reminded every citizen that rights and freedoms have a cost in bloodshed and struggle. When others, like the Taliban, sought to overthrow 226 years of progress in one bloody day, we relearned the most basic lesson of American citizenship—the price of citizenship is eternal vigilance.

The Constitution of the United States of America

NOTE: The following is a transcription of the Constitution in its original form. Items in italics have since been amended or superseded and are no longer in effect. Headings in parentheses are provided for clarification and indicate the purpose of each article or amendment.

PREAMBLE

We the People of the United States, in Order to form a more perfect Union, establish Justice, insure domestic Tranquility, provide for the common defense, promote the general Welfare, and secure the Blessings of Liberty to ourselves and our Posterity, do ordain and establish this Constitution for the United States of America.

ARTICLE. I. (Legislature)

Section. 1. All legislative Powers herein granted shall be vested in a Congress of the United States, which shall consist of a Senate and House of Representatives.

Section. 2. The House of Representatives shall be composed of Members chosen every second Year by the People of the several States, and the Electors in each State shall have the Qualifications requisite for Electors of the most numerous Branch of the State Legislature.

No Person shall be a Representative who shall not have attained to the Age of twenty five Years, and been seven Years a Citizen of the United States, and who shall not, when elected, be an Inhabitant of that State in which he shall be chosen.

Representatives and direct Taxes shall be apportioned among the several States which may be included within this Union, according to their respective numbers, *which shall be determined by adding to the whole Number of free Persons, including those bound to Service for a Term of Years and excluding Indians not taxed, three fifths of all other Persons.* The actual Enumeration shall be made within three Years after the first Meeting of the Congress of the United States, and within every subsequent Term of ten Years, in such Manner as they shall by Law direct. The Number of Representatives shall not exceed one for every thirty Thousand, but each State shall have at Least one Representative; *and until such enumeration shall be made, the State of New Hampshire shall be entitled to choose three, Massachusetts eight, Rhode Island and Providence Plantations one, Connecticut five, New York six, New Jersey four, Pennsylvania eight, Delaware one, Maryland six, Virginia ten, North Carolina five, South Carolina five, and Georgia three.*

When vacancies happen in the Representation from any State, the Executive Authority thereof shall issue Writs of Election to fill such Vacancies.

The House of Representatives shall choose their Speaker and other Officers; and shall have the sole Power of Impeachment.

Section. 3. The Senate of the United States shall be composed of two Senators from each State, *chosen by the Legislature thereof,* for six Years; and each Senator shall have one Vote.

Immediately after they shall be assembled in Consequence of the first Election, they shall be divided as equally as may be into three Classes. The Seats of the Senators of the first Class shall be vacated at the Expiration of the second Year, of the second Class at the Expiration of the fourth Year, and of the third Class at the Expiration of the sixth Year, so that one third may be chosen every second Year; *and if Vacancies happen by Resignation, or otherwise, during the Recess of the Legislature of any State, the Executive thereof may make temporary Appointments until the next Meeting of the Legislature, which shall then fill such Vacancies.*

No Person shall be a Senator who shall not have attained to the Age of thirty Years, and been nine Years a Citizen of the United States, and who shall not, when elected, be an Inhabitant of that State for which he shall be chosen.

The Vice President of the United States shall be President of the Senate, but shall have no Vote, unless they be equally divided.

The Senate shall choose their other Officers, and also a President pro tempore, in the Absence of the Vice President, or when he shall exercise the Office of President of the United States.

The Senate shall have the sole Power to try all Impeachments. When sitting for that Purpose, they shall be on Oath or Affirmation. When the President of the United States is tried, the Chief Justice shall preside: And no Person shall be convicted without the Concurrence of two thirds of the Members present.

Judgment in Cases of Impeachment shall not extend further than to removal from the Office, and disqualification to hold and enjoy any Office of honor, Trust or Profit under the United States: but the Party convicted shall nevertheless be liable and subject to Indictment, Trial, Judgment and Punishment, according to Law.

Section. 4. The Times, Places and Manner of holding Elections for Senators and Representatives, shall be prescribed in each State by the Legislature thereof; but the Congress may at any time by Law make or alter such Regulations, except as to the Places of choosing Senators.

The Congress shall assemble at least once in every Year, and such Meeting shall be *on the first Monday in December,* unless they shall by Law appoint a different Day.

Section. 5. Each House shall be the Judge of the Elections, Returns and Qualifications of its own Members, and a Majority of each shall constitute a Quorum to do Business; but a smaller Number may adjourn from day to day, and may be authorized to compel the Attendance of absent Members, in such Manner, and under such Penalties, as each House may provide.

Each House may determine the Rules of its Proceedings, punish its Members for disorderly Behavior, and, with the Concurrence of two thirds, expel a Member.

Each House shall keep a Journal of its Proceedings, and from time to time publish the same, excepting such Parts as may in their Judgment require Secrecy; and the Yeas and Nays of the Members of either House on any question shall, at the Desire of one fifth of those Present, be entered on the Journal.

Neither House, during the Session of Congress, shall, without the Consent of the other, adjourn for more than three days, nor to any other Place than that in which the two Houses shall be sitting.

Section 6. The Senators and Representatives shall receive a Compensation for their Services, to be ascertained by Law, and paid out of the Treasury of the United States. They shall in all Cases, except Treason, Felony and Breach of the Peace, be privileged from Arrest during their Attendance at the Session of their respective Houses, and in going to and returning from the same; and for any Speech or Debate in either House, they shall not be questioned in any other Place.

No Senator or Representative shall, during the Time for which he was elected, be appointed to any civil Office under the Authority of the United States, which shall have been created, or the Emoluments whereof shall have been increased during such time; and no Person holding any Office under the United States, shall be a Member of either House during his Continuance in Office.

Section. 7. All Bills for raising Revenue shall originate in the House of Representatives; but the Senate may propose or concur with Amendments as on other Bills.

Every Bill which shall have passed the House of Representatives and the Senate, shall, before it become a Law, be presented to the President of the United States: If he approve he shall sign it, but if not he shall return it, with his Objections to that House in which it shall have originated, who shall enter the Objections at large on their Journal, and proceed to reconsider it. If after such Reconsideration two thirds of that House shall agree to pass the Bill, it shall be sent, together with the Objections, to the other House, by which it shall likewise be reconsidered, and if approved by two thirds of that House, it shall become a Law. But in all such Cases the Votes of both Houses shall be determined by yeas and Nays, and the Names of the Persons voting for and against the Bill shall be entered on the Journal of each House respectively. If any Bill shall not be returned by the President within ten Days (Sundays excepted) after it shall have been presented to him, the Same shall be a Law, in like Manner as if he had signed it, unless the Congress by their Adjournment prevent its Return, in which Case it shall not be a Law.

Every Order, Resolution, or Vote to which the Concurrence of the Senate and House of Representatives may be necessary (except on a question of Adjournment) shall be presented to the President of the United States; and before the Same shall take Effect, shall be approved by him, or being disapproved by him, shall be repassed by two thirds of the Senate and House of Representatives, according to the Rules and Limitations prescribed in the Case of a Bill.

Section. 8. The Congress shall have Power:

To lay and collect Taxes, Duties, Imposts, and Excises, to pay the Debts and provide for the common Defense and general Welfare of the United States; but all Duties, Imposts and Excises shall be uniform throughout the United States;

To borrow Money on the credit of the United States;

To regulate Commerce with foreign Nations, and among the several States, and with the Indian Tribes;

To establish an uniform Rule of Naturalization, and uniform Laws on the subject of Bankruptcies throughout the United States;

To coin Money, regulate the Value thereof, and of

foreign Coin, and fix the Standard of Weights and Measures;

To provide for the Punishment of counterfeiting the Securities and current Coin of the United States;

To establish Post Offices and post Roads;

To promote the Progress of Science and useful Arts, by securing for limited Times to Authors and Inventors the exclusive Right to their respective Writings and Discoveries;

To constitute Tribunals inferior to the supreme Court;

To define and punish Piracies and Felonies committed on the high Seas and Offenses against the Law of Nations;

To declare War, grant Letters of Marque and Reprisal, and make Rules concerning Captures on Land and Water;

To raise and support Armies, but no Appropriation of Money to that Use shall be for a longer Term than two Years;

To provide and maintain a Navy;

To make Rules for the Government and Regulation of the land and naval Forces;

To provide for calling forth the Militia to execute the Laws of the Union, suppress Insurrections and repel Invasions;

To provide for organizing, arming, and disciplining, the Militia, and for governing such Part of them as may be employed in the Service of the United States, reserving to the States respectively, the Appointment of the Officers, and the Authority of training the Militia according to the discipline prescribed by Congress;

To exercise exclusive Legislation in all Cases whatsoever, over such District (not exceeding ten Miles square) as may, by Cession of particular States, and the Acceptance of Congress, become the Seat of the Government of the United States, and to exercise like Authority over all Places purchased by the Consent of the Legislature of the State in which the Same shall be, for the Erection of Forts, Magazines, Arsenals, dock-Yards, and other needful Buildings;—And

To make all Laws which shall be necessary and proper for carrying into Execution the foregoing Powers, and all other Powers vested by this Constitution in the Government of the United States, or in any Department or Officer thereof.

Section. 9. *The Migration or Importation of such Persons as any of the States now existing shall think proper to admit, shall not be prohibited by the Congress prior to the Year one thousand eight hundred and eight,* *but a Tax or duty may be imposed on such Importation, not exceeding ten dollars for each Person.*

The Privilege of the Writ of Habeas Corpus shall not be suspended, unless when in Cases of Rebellion or Invasion the public Safety may require it.

No Bill of Attainder or ex post facto Law shall be passed.

No Capitation or other direct, Tax shall be laid, *unless in Proportion to the Census or enumeration herein before directed to be taken.*

No Tax or Duty shall be laid on Articles exported from any State.

No Preference shall be given by any Regulation of Commerce or Revenue to the Ports of one State over those of another; nor shall Vessels bound to, or from, one State, be obliged to enter, clear, or pay Duties in another.

No Money shall be drawn from the Treasury, but in Consequence of Appropriations made by Law; and a regular Statement and Account of the Receipts and Expenditures of all public Money shall be published from time to time.

No Title of Nobility shall be granted by the United States: And no Person holding any Office of Profit or Trust under them, shall, without the Consent of the Congress, accept of any present, Emolument, Office, or Title, of any kind whatever, from any King, Prince, or foreign State.

Section. 10. No State shall enter into any Treaty, Alliance, or Confederation; grant Letters of Marque and Reprisal; coin Money, emit Bills of Credit; make any Thing but gold and silver Coin a Tender in Payment of Debts; pass any Bill of Attainder, ex post facto Law, or Law impairing the Obligation of Contracts, or grant any Title of Nobility.

No States shall, without the Consent of the Congress, lay any Imposts or Duties on Imports or Exports, except what may be absolutely necessary for executing its inspection Laws: and the net Produce of all Duties and Imposts, laid by any State on Imports or Exports, shall be for the Use of the Treasury of the United States; and all such Laws shall be subject to the Revision and Control of the Congress.

No State shall, without the Consent of Congress, lay any Duty of Tonnage, keep Troops, or Ships of War in time of Peace, enter into any Agreement or Compact with another State, or with a foreign Power, or engage in War, unless actually invaded, or in such imminent Danger as will not admit of delay.

ARTICLE. II.   (Executive; President)

Section. 1. The executive Power shall be vested in a President of the United States of America. He shall hold his Office during the Term of four Years, and, together with the Vice President, chosen for the same Term, be elected, as follows:

Each State shall appoint, in such Manner as the Legislature thereof may direct, a Number of Electors, equal to the whole Number of Senators and Representatives to which the State may be entitled in the Congress; but no Senator or Representative, or Person holding an Office of Trust or Profit under the United States, shall be appointed an Elector.

The Electors shall meet in their respective States, and vote by Ballot for two Persons, of whom one at least shall not be an Inhabitant of the same State with themselves. And they shall make a List of all the Persons voted for, and of the Number of Votes for each; which List they shall sign and certify, and transmit sealed to the Seat of the Government of the United States, directed to the President of the Senate. The President of the Senate shall, in the Presence of the Senate and House of Representatives, open all the Certificates, and the Votes shall then be counted. The Person having the greatest Number of Votes shall be the President, if such Number be a Majority of the whole Number of Electors appointed; and if there be more than one who have such Majority, and have an equal Number of Votes, then the House of Representatives shall immediately choose by Ballot one of them for President; and if no Person have a Majority, then from the five highest on the List said House shall in like Manner choose the President. But in choosing the President, the Votes shall be taken by States, the Representation from each State having one Vote; A quorum for this purpose shall consist of a Member or Members from two thirds of the States, and a Majority of all the States shall be necessary to a Choice. In every Case, after the Choice of the President, the Person having the greatest Number of Votes of the electors shall be the Vice President. But if there should remain two or more who have equal Votes, the Senate shall choose from them by Ballot the Vice President.

The Congress may determine the Time of choosing the Electors, and the Day on which they shall give their Votes; which Day shall be the same throughout the United States.

No Person except a natural born Citizen, *or a Citizen of the United States at the time of the Adoption of this Constitution,* shall be eligible to the Office of President; neither shall any Person be eligible to that Office who shall not have attained to the Age of thirty five Years, and been fourteen Years a Resident within the United States.

In Case of the Removal of the President from Office, or of his Death, Resignation, or Inability to discharge the Powers and Duties of the said Office, the Same shall devolve on the Vice President, and the Congress may by Law provide for the Case of Removal, Death, Resignation or Inability, both of the President and Vice President, declaring what Officer shall then act as President, and such Officer shall act accordingly, until the Disability be removed, or a President shall be elected.

The President shall, at stated Times, receive for his Services, a Compensation, which shall neither be increased nor diminished during the Period for which he shall have been elected, and he shall not receive within that Period any other Emolument from the United States, or any of them.

Before he enter on the Execution of his Office, he shall take the following Oath or Affirmation:—"I do solemnly swear (or affirm) that I will faithfully execute the Office of President of the United States, and will to the best of my Ability, preserve, protect and defend the Constitution of the United States."

Section. 2. The President shall be Commander in Chief of the Army and Navy of the United States, and of the Militia of the several States, when called into the actual Service of the United States; he may require the Opinion, in writing, of the principal Officer in each of the executive Departments, upon any Subject relating to the Duties of their respective Offices, and he shall have Power to grant Reprieves and Pardons for Offenses against the United States, except in Cases of Impeachment.

He shall have Power, by and with the Advice and Consent of the Senate, to make Treaties, provided two thirds of the Senators present concur; and he shall nominate, and by and with the Advice and Consent of the Senate, shall appoint Ambassadors, other public Ministers and Consuls, Judges of the supreme Court, and all other Officers of the United States, whose Appointments are not herein otherwise provided for, and which shall be established by Law: but the Congress may by Law vest the Appointment of such inferior Officers, as they think proper, in the President alone, in the Courts of Law, or in the Heads of Departments.

The President shall have Power to fill up all Vacancies that may happen during the Recess of the Senate, by granting Commissions which shall expire at the End of their next session.

Section. 3. He shall from time to time give to the Congress Information of the State of the Union, and recommend to their Consideration such Measures as he shall judge necessary and expedient; he may, on extraordinary Occasions, convene both Houses, or either of them, and in Case of Disagreement between them, with Respect to the Time of Adjournment, he may adjourn them to such Time as he shall think proper; he shall receive Ambassadors and other public Ministers; he shall take Care that the Laws be faithfully executed, and shall Commission all the Officers of the United States.

Section. 4. The President, Vice President and all civil Officers of the United States, shall be removed from Office on Impeachment for, and Conviction of, Treason, Bribery, or other high Crimes and Misdemeanors.

ARTICLE. III.   (Judiciary)

Section. 1. The judicial Power of the United States shall be vested in one supreme Court, and in such inferior Courts as the Congress may from time to time ordain and establish. The Judges, both of the supreme and inferior Courts, shall hold their Offices during good Behavior, and shall, at stated Times, receive for their Services a Compensation, which shall not be diminished during their Continuance in Office.

Section 2. The judicial Power shall extend to all Cases, in Law and Equity, arising under this Constitution, the Laws of the United States, and Treaties made, or which shall be made, under their Authority—to all Cases affecting Ambassadors, other public Ministers and Consuls;—to all Cases of admiralty and maritime Jurisdiction;—to Controversies to which the United States shall be a party;—to controversies between two or more States;—*between a State and Citizens of another State;*—between Citizens of different States;—between Citizens of the same State claiming Lands under Grants of different States, and between a State, or the Citizens thereof, and foreign States, Citizens or Subjects.

In all Cases affecting Ambassadors, other public Ministers and Consuls, and those in which a State shall be Party, the supreme Court shall have original Jurisdiction. In all the other Cases before mentioned, the supreme Court shall have appellate Jurisdiction, both as to Law and Fact, with such Exceptions, and under such Regulations as the Congress shall make.

The Trial of all Crimes, except in Cases of Impeachment, shall be by Jury; and such Trial shall be held in the State where said Crimes shall have been committed; but when not committed within any State, the Trial shall be at such Place or Places as the Congress may by Law have directed.

Section 3. Treason against the United States, shall consist only in levying War against them, or in adhering to their Enemies, giving them Aid and Comfort. No Person shall be convicted of Treason unless on the Testimony of two Witnesses to the same overt Act, or on Confession in open Court.

The Congress shall have Power to declare the Punishment of Treason, but no Attainder of Treason shall work Corruption of Blood, or Forfeiture except during the Life of the Person attainted.

ARTICLE. IV.   (Federal System)

Section. 1. Full Faith and Credit shall be given in each State to the public Acts, Records, and judicial Proceedings of every other State. And the Congress may by general Laws prescribe the Manner in which such Acts, Records and Proceedings shall be proved, and the Effect thereof.

Section. 2. The Citizens of each State shall be entitled to all Privileges and Immunities of Citizens in the several States.

A Person charged in any State with Treason, Felony, or other Crime, who shall flee from Justice, and be found in another State, shall on Demand of the executive Authority of the State from which he fled, be delivered up, to be removed to the State having Jurisdiction of the crime.

No Person held to Service or Labour in one State, under the Laws thereof, escaping into another, shall, in Consequence of any Law or Regulation therein, be discharged from such Service or Labour, but shall be delivered up on Claim of the Party to whom such Service or Labour may be due.

Section. 3. New States may be admitted by the Congress into this Union; but no new State shall be formed or erected within the Jurisdiction of any other State; nor any State be formed by the Junction of two or more States, or Parts of States, without the Consent of the Legislatures of the States concerned as well as of the Congress.

The Congress shall have Power to dispose of and make all needful Rules and Regulations respecting the Territory or other Property belonging to the United States; and nothing in this Constitution shall be so construed as to Prejudice any Claims of the United States, or of any particular State.

Section. 4. The United States shall guarantee to every State in this Union a Republican Form of Government, and shall protect each of them against Invasion; and on Application of the Legislature, or of the Executive (when the Legislature cannot be convened), against domestic Violence.

ARTICLE. V.   (Amendments)

The Congress, whenever two thirds of both Houses shall deem it necessary, shall propose Amendments to this Constitution, or, on the Application of the Legislatures of two thirds of the several States, shall call a Convention for proposing Amendments, which, in either Case, shall be valid to all Intents and Purposes, as Part of this Constitution, when ratified by the Legislatures of three fourths of the several States, or by Conventions in three fourths thereof, as the one or the other Mode of Ratification may be proposed by the Congress; Provided *that no Amendment which may be made prior to the Year One thousand eight hundred and eight shall in any Manner affect the first and fourth Clauses in the Ninth Section of the first Article; and* that no State, without its Consent, shall be deprived of its equal Suffrage in the Senate.

ARTICLE. VI.   (Constitution as Supreme Law)

All Debts contracted and Engagements entered into, before the Adoption of this Constitution, shall be as valid against the United States under this Constitution, as under the Confederation.

This Constitution, and the Laws of the United States which shall be made in Pursuance thereof; and all Treaties made, or which shall be made, under the Authority of the United States, shall be the supreme Law of the Land, and the Judges in every State shall be bound thereby, any Thing in the Constitution or Laws of any State to the Contrary notwithstanding.

The Senators and Representatives before mentioned, and the Members of the several State Legislatures, and all executive and judicial Officers, both of the United States and of the several States, shall be bound by Oath or Affirmation, to support this Constitution; but no religious Test shall ever be required as a Qualification to any Office or public Trust under the United States.

ARTICLE. VII.   (Ratification)

The Ratification of the Conventions of nine States, shall be sufficient for the Establishment of this Constitution between the States so ratifying the Same.

Attest William Jackson, *Secretary*

Done in Convention by the Unanimous Consent of the States present the Seventeenth Day of September in the Year of our Lord one thousand seven hundred and Eighty seven and of the Independence of the United States of America the twelfth. In witness whereof We have hereunto subscribed our Names,

Go. Washington, *President and deputy from Virginia;*
Delaware: Geo. Read, Gunning Bedford, Jr., John Dickinson, Richard Bassett, Jaco. Broom;
Maryland: James McHenry, Daniel of St. Thomas' Jenifer, Danl. Carroll;
Virginia: John Blair, James Madison, Jr.;
North Carolina: Wm. Blount, Richd. Dobbs Spaight, Hu Williamson;
South Carolina: J. Rutledge, Charles Cotesworth Pinckney, Charles Pinckney, Pierce Butler;
Georgia: William Few, Abr. Baldwin;
New Hampshire: John Langdon, Nicholas Gilman;
Massachusetts: Nathaniel Gorham, Rufus King;
Connecticut: Wm. Saml. Johnson, Roger Sherman;
New York: Alexander Hamilton;
New Jersey: Wil. Livingston, David Brearley, Wm. Paterson, Jona. Dayton;
Pennsylvania: B. Franklin, Thomas Mifflin, Robt. Morris, Geo. Clymer, Thos. FitzSimons, Jared Ingersoll, James Wilson, Gouv. Morris.

Amendments to the Constitution

(The first ten amendments are known as The Bill of Rights.)

AMENDMENT I [1791]   *(Freedoms)*
(Religion, Speech, Press, Assembly, and Petition)

Congress shall make no law respecting an establishment of religion, or prohibiting the free exercise thereof, or abridging the freedom of speech, or of the press, or the right of the people peaceably to assemble, and to petition the Government for a redress of grievances.

AMENDMENT II [1791]   *(Right to Bear Arms)*

A well regulated Militia, being necessary to the security of a free State, the right of the people to keep and bear Arms, shall not be infringed.

AMENDMENT III [1791]   *(Quartering of Soldiers)*

No soldier shall, in time of peace be quartered in any house, without consent of the Owner, nor in time of war, but in a manner to be prescribed by law.

AMENDMENT IV [1791]   *(Freedom of Persons)*
(Warrants, Searches, and Seizure)

The right of the people to be secure in their persons, houses, papers, and effects, against unreasonable searches and seizures, shall not be violated, and no Warrants shall issue; but upon probable cause, supported by Oath or Affirmation, and particularly describing the place to be searched, and the persons or things to be seized.

AMENDMENT V [1791]   *(Capital Crimes)*
(Protection of the Accused; Compensation)

No person shall be held to answer for a capital, or otherwise infamous crime, unless on a presentment or indictment of a Grand Jury, except in cases arising in the land or naval forces, or in the Militia, when in actual service in time of War or public danger; nor shall any person be subject for the same offense to be twice put in jeopardy of life or limb, nor shall be compelled in any criminal case to be a witness against himself, nor be deprived of life, liberty, or property without due process of law; nor

shall private property be taken for public use, without just compensation.

AMENDMENT VI [1791]   *(Trial by Jury)*
(Accusation, Witnesses, Counsel)

In all criminal prosecutions, the accused shall enjoy the right to a speedy and public trial, by an impartial jury of the State and district wherein the crime shall have been committed, which district shall have been previously ascertained by law, and to be informed of the nature and cause of the accusation; to be confronted with the witnesses against him; to have compulsory process for obtaining Witnesses in his favor, and to have the Assistance of Counsel for his defense.

AMENDMENT VII [1791]   *(Civil Law)*

In Suits at common law, where the value in controversy shall exceed twenty dollars, the right of trial by jury shall be preserved, and no fact tried by a jury, shall be otherwise re-examined in any Court of the United States, than according to the rules of the common law.

AMENDMENT VIII [1791]   *(Bails, Fines, and Punishments)*

Excessive bail shall not be required, nor excessive fines imposed, nor cruel and unusual punishments inflicted.

AMENDMENT IX [1791]   *(Rights Retained by the People)*

The enumeration in the Constitution, of certain rights, shall not be construed to deny or disparage others retained by the people.

AMENDMENT X [1791]   *(Rights Reserved to the States)*

The powers not delegated to the United States by the Constitution, nor prohibited by it to the States, are reserved to the States respectively, or to the people.

AMENDMENT XI [1798]   *(Jurisdictional Limits)*

The judicial power of the United States shall not be construed to extend to any suit in law or equity, commenced or prosecuted against one of the United States by citizens of another State, or by citizens or subjects of any foreign state.

AMENDMENT XII [1804]   *(Electoral College)*

The Electors shall meet in their respective States, and vote by ballot for President and Vice President, one of whom, at least, shall not be an inhabitant of the same State with themselves; they shall name in their ballots the person voted for as President, and in distinct ballots the person voted for as Vice President, and they shall make distinct lists of all persons voted for as President, and of all persons voted for as Vice President, and of the number of votes for each, which lists they shall sign and certify, and transmit sealed to the seat of the government of the United States, directed to the President of the Senate; the President of the Senate shall, in the presence of the Senate and House of Representatives, open all the certificates and the votes shall then be counted;— The person having the greatest number of votes for President, shall be the President, if such number be a majority of the whole number of Electors appointed; and if no person have such majority, then from the persons having the highest numbers not exceeding three on the list of those voted for as President, the House of Representatives shall choose immediately, by ballot, the President. But in choosing the President, the votes shall be taken by States, the representation from each State having one vote; a quorum for this purpose shall consist of a member or members from two-thirds of the States, and a majority of all the States shall be necessary to a choice. *And if the House of Representatives shall not choose a President whenever the right of choice shall devolve upon them, before the fourth day of March next following, then the Vice President shall act as President, as in the case of the death or other constitutional disability of the President.*

The person having the greatest number of votes as Vice President, shall be the Vice President, if such number be a majority of the whole number of Electors appointed; and if no person have a majority, then from the two highest numbers on the list, the Senate shall choose the Vice President; a quorum for the purpose shall consist of two-thirds of the whole number of Senators, and a majority of the whole number shall be necessary to a choice. But no person constitutionally ineligible to the office of President shall be eligible to that of Vice President of the United States.

AMENDMENT XIII [1865]   *(Abolition of Slavery)*

Section 1. Neither slavery nor involuntary servitude, except as a punishment for crime whereof the party shall have been duly convicted, shall exist within the United States or any place subject to their jurisdiction.

Section 2. Congress shall have power to enforce this article by appropriate legislation.

AMENDMENT XIV [1868]   *(Citizenship)*
(Due Process of Law)

Section 1. All persons born or naturalized in the United States, and subject to the jurisdiction thereof, are citizens of the United States and of the State wherein they reside. No State shall make or enforce any law which shall abridge the privileges or immunities of citizens of the United States; nor shall any State deprive any person of life, liberty, or property, without due process of law; nor deny to any person within its jurisdiction the equal protection of the laws.

(Apportionment; Right to Vote)
Section 2. Representatives shall be apportioned among the several States according to their respective numbers, counting the whole number of persons in each State, excluding Indians not taxed. But when the right to vote at any election for the choice of Electors for President and Vice President of the United States, Representatives in Congress, the executive and judicial officers of a State, or the members of the Legislature thereof, is denied to any of the male inhabitants of such State, being twenty-one years of age, and, citizens of the United States, or in any way abridged, except for participation in rebellion, or other crime, the basis of representation therein shall be reduced in the proportion which the number of such male citizens shall bear to the whole number of male citizens twenty-one years of age in such State.

(Disqualification for Office)
Section 3. No person shall be a Senator or Representative in Congress, or Elector of President and Vice President, or hold any office, civil or military, under the United States, or under any State, who, having previously taken an oath, as a member of Congress, or as an officer of the United States, or as a member of any State

Legislature, or as an executive or judicial officer of any State, to support the Constitution of the United States, shall have engaged in insurrection or rebellion against the same, or given aid or comfort to the enemies thereof. But Congress may by a vote of two-thirds of each House, remove such disability.

(Public Debt)

Section 4. The validity of the public debt of the United States, authorized by law, including debts incurred for payment of pensions and bounties for services in suppressing insurrection or rebellion, shall not be questioned. But neither the United States nor any State shall assume or pay any debt or obligation incurred in aid of insurrection or rebellion against the United States, or any claim for the loss of emancipation of any slave; but all such debts, obligations and claims, shall be held illegal and void.

Section 5. The Congress shall have power to enforce, by appropriate legislation, the provisions of this article.

AMENDMENT XV [1870]   *(Right to Vote)*

Section 1. The right of citizens of the United States to vote shall not be denied or abridged by the United States or by any State on account of race, color, or previous condition of servitude.

Section 2. The Congress shall have power to enforce this article by appropriate legislation.

AMENDMENT XVI [1913]   *(Income Tax)*

The Congress shall have power to lay and collect taxes on incomes, from whatever source derived, without apportionment among the several States, and without regard to any census or enumeration.

AMENDMENT XVII [1913]   *(Senators)*
                                    (Election)

Section 1. The Senate of the United States shall be composed of two Senators from each State, elected by the people thereof, for six years; and each Senator shall have one vote. The electors in each State shall have the qualifications requisite for electors of [voters for] the most numerous branch of the State Legislatures.

(Vacancies)

Section 2. When vacancies happen in the representation of any State in the Senate, the executive authority of such State shall issue writs of election to fill such vacancies: Provided, That the Legislature of any State may empower the Executive thereof to make temporary appointments until the people fill the vacancies by election as the Legislature may direct.

Section 3. This amendment shall not be so construed as to affect the election or term of any Senator chosen before it becomes valid as part of the Constitution.

AMENDMENT XVIII [1919]   *(Prohibition)*

Section 1. After one year from the ratification of this article the manufacture, sale, or transportation of intoxicating liquors within, the importation thereof into, or the exportation thereof from the United States and all territory subject to the jurisdiction thereof for beverage purposes is hereby prohibited.

Section 2. The Congress and the several States shall have concurrent power to enforce this article by appropriate legislation.

Section 3. This article shall be inoperative unless it shall have been ratified as an amendment to the Constitution by the Legislatures of the several States, as provided in the Constitution, within seven years from the date of the submission thereof to the States by the Congress.

AMENDMENT XIX [1920]   *(Women's Suffrage)*

Section 1. The right of citizens of the United States to vote shall not be denied or abridged by the United States or by any State on account of sex.

Section 2. Congress shall have power to enforce this Article by appropriate legislation.

AMENDMENT XX [1933]   *(Terms of Office)*

Section 1. The terms of the President and Vice President shall end at noon on the 20th day of January, and the terms of Senators and Representatives at noon on the 3rd day of January, of the years in which such terms would have ended if this article had not been ratified; and the terms of their successors shall then begin.

Section 2. The Congress shall assemble at least once in every year, and such meeting shall begin at noon on the 3rd day of January, unless they shall by law appoint a different day.

(Succession)

Section 3. If, at the time fixed for the beginning of the term of the President, the President-elect shall have died, the Vice President-elect shall become President. If a President shall not have been chosen before the time fixed for the beginning of his term, or if the President-elect shall have failed to qualify, then the Vice President-elect shall act as President until a President shall have qualified; and the Congress may by law provide for the case wherein neither a President-elect nor a Vice President-elect shall have qualified, declaring who shall then act as President, or the manner in which one who is to act shall be selected, and such persons shall act accordingly until a President or Vice President shall have qualified.

Section 4. The Congress may by law provide for the case of the death of any of the persons from whom the House of Representatives may choose a President whenever the right of choice shall have devolved upon them, and for the case of the death of any of the persons from whom the Senate may choose a Vice President whenever the right of choice shall have devolved upon them.

Section 5. Sections 1 and 2 shall take effect on the 15th day of October following the ratification of this article.

Section 6. This article shall be inoperative unless it shall have been ratified as an amendment to the Constitution by the Legislatures of three-fourths of the several States within seven years from the date of its submission.

AMENDMENT XXI [1933] *(Prohibition Repealed)*

Section 1. The eighteenth article of amendment to the Constitution of the United States is hereby repealed.

Section 2. The transportation or importation into any State, Territory, or Possession of the United States for delivery or use therein of intoxicating liquors, in violation of the laws thereof, is hereby prohibited.

Section 3. This article shall be inoperative unless it shall have been ratified as an amendment to the Constitution by conventions in the several States, as provided in the Constitution, within seven years from the date of submission thereof to the States by the Congress.

AMENDMENT XXII [1951] *(Term of President)*

Section 1. No person shall be elected to the office of the President more than twice, and no person who has held the office of President, or acted as President, for more than two years of a term to which some other person was elected President shall be elected to the office of President more than once. But this Article shall not apply to any person holding the office of President when this Article was proposed by the Congress, and shall not prevent any person who may be holding the office of President, or acting as President, during the term within which this Article becomes operative from holding the office of President or acting as President during the remainder of such term.

Section 2. This article shall be inoperative unless it shall have been ratified as an amendment to the Constitution by the Legislatures of three-fourths of the several States within seven years from the date of its submission to the States by the Congress.

AMENDMENT XXIII [1961] *(Washington, D.C.)*
(Enfranchisement of Voters in Federal Elections)

Section 1. The District constituting the seat of Government of the United States shall appoint in such manner as the Congress may direct:

A number of electors of President and Vice President equal to the whole number of Senators and Representatives in Congress to which the District would be entitled if it were a State, but in no event more than the least populous State; they shall be in addition to those appointed by the States, but they shall be considered, for the purposes of the election of President and Vice President, to be electors appointed by a State; and they shall meet in the District and perform such duties as provided by the twelfth article of amendment.

Section 2. The Congress shall have power to enforce this article by appropriate legislation.

AMENDMENT XXIV [1964] *(Poll Tax)*

Section 1. The right of citizens of the United States to vote in any primary or other election for President or Vice President, for electors for President or Vice President, or for Senator or Representative in Congress, shall not be denied or abridged by the United States or any State by reason of failure to pay any poll tax or other tax.

Section 2. The Congress shall have power to enforce this article by appropriate legislation.

AMENDMENT XXV [1967]   *(Succession)*

Section 1. In case of the removal of the President from office or of his death or resignation, the Vice President shall become President.

Section 2. Whenever there is a vacancy in the office of the Vice President, the President shall nominate a Vice President who shall take office upon confirmation by a majority vote of both houses of Congress.

Section 3. Whenever the President transmits to the President pro tempore of the Senate and the Speaker of the House of Representatives his written declaration that he is unable to discharge the power and duties of his office, and until he transmits to them a written declaration to the contrary, such powers and duties shall be discharged by the Vice President as Acting President.

Section 4. Whenever the Vice President and a majority of either the principal officers of the executive departments or of such other body as Congress may by law provide, transmit to the President pro tempore of the Senate and the Speaker of the House of Representatives their written declaration that the President is unable to discharge the powers and duties of his office, the Vice President shall immediately assume the powers and duties of the office as Acting President.

Thereafter, when the President transmits to the President pro tempore of the Senate and the Speaker of the House of Representatives his written declaration that no inability exists, he shall resume the powers and duties of his office unless the Vice President and a majority of either the principal officers of the executive departments or of such other body as Congress may by law provide, transmit within four days to the President pro tempore of the Senate and the Speaker of the House of Representatives their written declaration that the President is unable to discharge the powers and duties of his office. Thereupon Congress shall decide the issue, assembling within forty-eight hours for that purpose if not in session. If the Congress, within twenty-one days after receipt of the latter written declaration, or, if Congress is not in session, within twenty-one days after Congress is required to assemble, determines by two-thirds vote of both Houses that the President is unable to discharge the powers and duties of his office, the Vice President shall continue to discharge the same as Acting President; otherwise, the President shall resume the powers and duties of his office.

AMENDMENT XXVI [1971]   *(18-Year-Old Vote)*

Section 1. The right of citizens of the United States, who are eighteen years of age or older, to vote shall not be denied or abridged by the United States or by any State on account of age.

Section 2. The Congress shall have power to enforce this article by appropriate legislation.

AMENDMENT XXVII [1992]   *(Congressional Pay Raises)*

No law, varying the compensation for the services of the Senators and Representatives, shall take effect, until an election of Representatives shall have intervened.

Answer Keys

The U.S. Constitution: Word Search (p. 7)

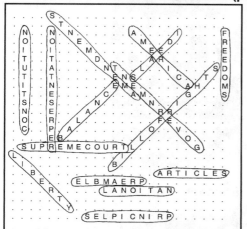

The Principles of Government: Cryptogram (p. 17)

1. Preamble
2. Constitution
3. Bill of Rights
4. Concurrent
5. Act of Congress
6. Founding Fathers
7. Equality
8. Amendments
9. Rule of Law
10. Popular rule
11. Constituency
12. Articles

Elections: Word Search (p. 22)

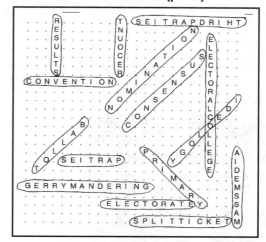

The U.S. Constitution: Kriss Kross (p. 8)

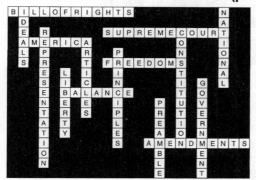

Which Is Which?: The Bill of Rights (p. 13)

1. 1	2. 1	3. 0	4. 4
5. 6	6. 8	7. 2	8. 1
9. 5	10. 5, 6	11. 10	12. 10
13. 1	14. 4, 5, 6	15. 1	16. 1
17. 0	18. 8	19. 1	20. 1

Campaigns: Kriss Kross (p. 26)

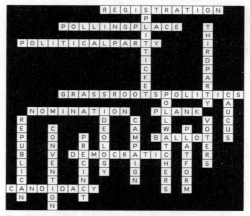

Federalism: Word Search (p. 16)

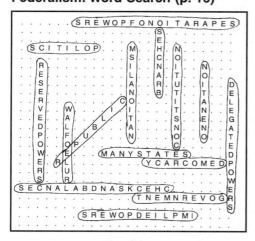

Political Parties: Word Search (p. 31)

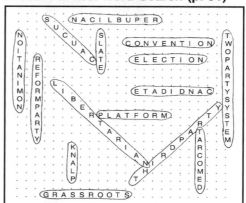

The Legislative Branch: Word Search (p. 34)

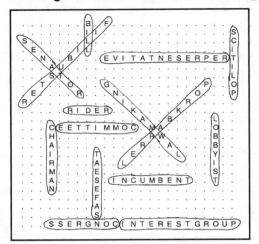

Congress: Kriss Kross (p. 39)

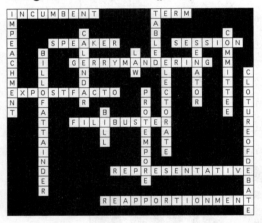

The Judicial Branch: Word Search (p. 43)

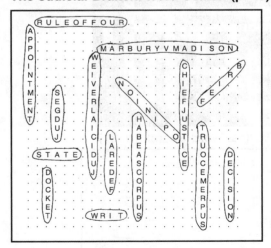

The Federal Court System: Kriss Kross (p. 44)

The Executive Branch: Kriss Kross (p. 47)

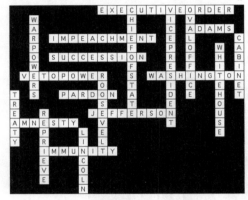

The American Flag: Vital Facts (p. 48)

1. Original 13 states (colonies)
2. Red = Courage   White = Purity
   Blue = Justice, Vigilance
3. Sunrise to sunset
4. Water
5. Distress
6. "Old Glory"
7. A new star was added for each new state.
8. Stand at attention, hand over heart
9. None. All flags stay at the same height.
10. Betsy Ross
11. It was a motto found on an early colonial flag.
12. Spotlighted
13. "The Star-Spangled Banner"

The Executive Departments: Word Scrambler (p. 50)

1. Education	2. State
3. Commerce	4. Veterans Affairs
5. Justice	6. Urban Development
7. Agriculture	8. Treasury
9. Defense	10. Interior
11. Health	12. Energy
13. Labor	14. Transportation
15. Armed Forces	16. Executive Branch
17. Human Services	18. Departments
19. Housing	20. Homeland Security

Bits and Pieces of Politics (p. 52)

1. The Liberty Bell
2. John Adams and George Bush
3. President Lincoln ordered the arrest of the state legislators.
4. Herbert Hoover
5. Carol Moseley-Braun
6. Pennsylvania
7. President Dwight D. Eisenhower
8. George Wallace
9. William Henry Harrison
10.
    A. He delivered a 105-minute speech at his inauguration.
    B. He was the first president to die in office (pneumonia).
    C. He only served one month in office.
11. She was the first woman to receive an electoral vote in the 1972 election (vice-presidential candidate).

Running the Country: Word Search (p. 56)

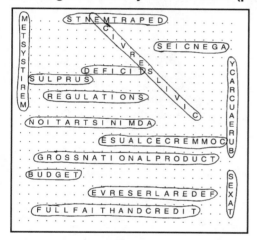

Sense and Nonsense (p. 59)

1. There are nine justices, not ten.
2. Democracy means that NO ONE is above the law.
3. The Bill of Rights DOES NOT state that the government is always supreme.
4. Under federalism, a state is not as powerful as the national government.
5. Elections cannot be held at any time.
6. Political third parties are usually unsuccessful.
7. The courts do not enforce the laws; they interpret them.
8. A president has no authority to filibuster.
9. The Cabinet cannot hold a "caucus on Congress."
10. A president may not gerrymander anyone.
11. A writ of certiorari requests the transcripts of a case.
12. No court has jurisdiction over all types of cases.

State Government: Kriss Kross (p. 62)

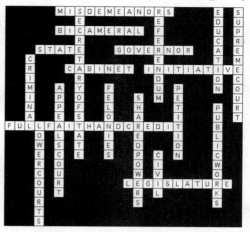

Local Government: Word Scrambler (p. 67)

1. Mayor
2. District
3. Municipalities
4. County
5. Village
6. Voter registration
7. Jails
8. Charter
9. Prosecutor
10. Commissioner
11. Sheriff
12. Coroner
13. City Manager
14. Council
15. Collector

Principles of Government: Master Blaster Crossword (p. 71)

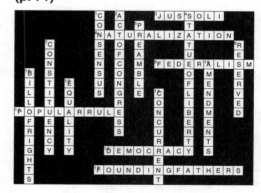

Branches of Government: Master Blaster Crossword (p. 72)

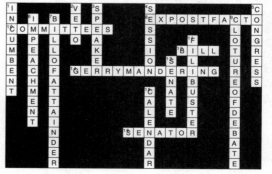

Campaigns, Parties, Elections: Master Blaster Crossword (p. 73)

American Government: Grand Master Word Search (p. 74)

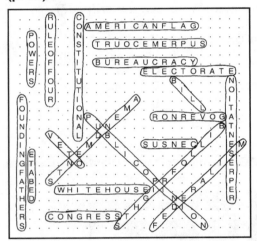

American Government: Grand Master Kriss Kross (p. 75)

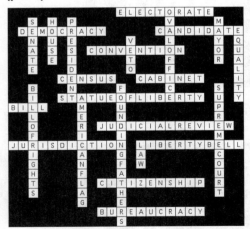

Bibliography

Baker, Richard A. *The Senate of the United States*. Krieger, 1988.

Bardes, Barbara A., Mack Shelley II, Steffen W. Schmitt. *American Government and Politics Today: The Essentials*, 10th ed. Wadsworth Publishing Company, 2002.

Baum, Lawrence. *American Courts: Process and Policy*, 2nd ed. Houghton Mifflin, 1990.

Bookchin, Murray. *The Rise of Urbanization and the Decline of Citizenship*. Sierra Club Books, 1987.

Bernstein, Robert A. *Elections and Representations*. Prentice-Hall, 1989.

Cummings, Milton C. Jr. and David Wise. *Democracy Under Pressure: An Introduction to the American Political System*, 8th ed. Harcourt Brace Publishers, 1985.

Dye, Thomas. *Politics in America,* 4th ed. Prentice-Hall, 2002.

Evans, Lawrence C. *Leadership in Committee: A Comparative Analysis of Leadership in the U.S. Senate*. University of Michigan Press, 1991.

Gienapp, William E. *The Origins of the Republican Party, 1852–1856*. Oxford Press, 1988.

Gizzi, Michael C., Tracey Gladstone-Sovell, William Wilkerson. *The Web of Democracy: An Intro to American Politics*, 1st ed. Wadsworth Publishing Company, 2002.

Goehlert, Robert U. and Fenton S. Martin. *Congress and Law-Making*, 2nd ed. ABC-CLIO, 1985.

Goldman, Ralph M. *Dilemma and Destiny: The Democratic Party in America*. University of America Press, 1986.

Grigsby, Ellen. *Analyzing Politics: An Introduction to Political Science*, 2nd ed. Wadsworth Publishing Company, 2002.

Grofman, B. and A. Lijphart eds. *Electoral Laws and Their Political Consequences*. Agathon Press, 1985.

Hinckley, Barbara. *Stability and Change in Congress*, 4th ed. Harper Press, 1987.

Louch, Robert S. *State and Local Politics: The Great Entanglement*, 6th ed. Prentice-Hall, 2001.

Neiman, Max. *Defending Government: Why Big Government Works*, 1st ed. Prentice-Hall, 2000.

Ripley, Randall B. *The Congress: Process and Policy*. Norton Press, 1988.

Scholzman, Kay Lehman, ed. *Elections in America*. Allen & Unwin, 1987.

Taagepera, Rein and Matthew Shugart. *Seats and Votes*. Yale University Press, 1989.

Vogler, David J. *The Politics of Congress*, 5th ed. W.C. Brown, 1988.

Volkomer, Walter E. *American Government: Updated Election Edition*, 9th ed. Prentice-Hall, 2001.

Web Resource Bibliography

One of the fastest, most efficient methods for getting information on topics is the Internet. The list below is an excellent sampling of websites that will enable the reader to collect all sorts of useful and fun facts about American government.

www.:

firstgov.gov	Directory of resources
whitehouse.gov	The White House
gsa.gov	U.S. General Service Administration
senate.gov	U.S. Senate
house.gov	U.S. House of Representatives
fedstats.gov	Federal statistics
census.gov	U.S. Census
bea.doc/gov	Bureau of Economic Analysis
ojp.usdoj.gov	Department of Justice
usconstitution.net	Everything about the Constitution
govspot.com	Government resources/referrals
SpeakOut.com	Political activism
Politicalinformation.com	As the title suggests
Politics1.com	Web searcher/resource list
Aboutpolitics.com	Daily review of politics
politicalresources.net	As the title suggests
wheretodoresearch.com	Useful source for state government information
cnn.com/allpolitics	Daily report of political news
greatsource.com	Online almanac